Modern Critical Interpretations
John Steinbeck's
The Grapes of Wrath

Modern Critical Interpretations

These and other titles in preparation

John Steinbeck's
The Grapes of Wrath

Edited and with an introduction by

Harold Bloom
Sterling Professor of the Humanities
Yale University

Chelsea House Publishers
NEW YORK ◊ PHILADELPHIA

© 1988 by Chelsea House Publishers, a division of Main Line Book Co.

Introduction © 1987 by Harold Bloom

Printed and bound in the United States of America

10 9 8 7 6 5 4

∞ The paper used in this publication meets the minimum requirements of the American National Standard for Permanence of Paper for Printed Library Materials, Z39.48-1984.

Library of Congress Cataloging-in-Publication Data
John Steinbeck's The grapes of wrath / edited with an introduction by Harold Bloom.
    p. cm.—(Modern critical interpretations)
    Bibliography: p.
    Includes index.
    Summary: A collection of seven critical essays on Steinbeck's "The Grapes of Wrath" arranged in chronological order of publication.
    ISBN 1-55546-050-X
    1. Steinbeck, John, 1902–1968. Grapes of wrath. [1. Steinbeck, John, 1902–1968. Grapes of wrath. 2. American literature—History and criticism.] I. Bloom, Harold. II. Series.
PS3537.T3234G856 1988
813'.52—dc19
                                      87–22187
                                        CIP
                                        AC

Contents

Editor's Note

This book brings together a representative selection of the best critical interpretations of John Steinbeck's major novel *The Grapes of Wrath*. The critical essays are reprinted here in the chronological order of their original publication. I am grateful to James Swenson for his aid in editing this volume.

My introduction considers Hemingway's influence upon Steinbeck, and then seeks to define both the limitations and the lasting value of *The Grapes of Wrath*. Frederic I. Carpenter begins the chronological sequence of criticism with a philosophical defense of Steinbeck's novel, relating it to Emerson, Whitman, and American Pragmatism.

In Howard Levant's reading, the novel is regarded as a mature prose epic successful on its own terms for its first three quarters, but then yielding to flaws in its final portion. The influence of Ecclesiastes and its skepticism upon *The Grapes of Wrath* is traced by James D. Brasch.

Floyd C. Watkins reproves Steinbeck for writing about Okies, a people he did not know, thus mistaking their culture and their religion. Different limitations are explored by Sylvia Jenkins Cook, who finds *The Grapes of Wrath* nothing new, but only the culmination of the old literature of the Left.

Donald Pizer finds it is the Joads themselves, and not their "thoughts," that constitute the enduring element in the novel. This is akin to the analysis of John J. Conder, who sees *The Grapes of Wrath* as an Emersonian instance of the self being both determined by nature and also transcending nature. In this volume's final essay, Mimi Reisel Gladstein contrasts Steinbeck's "primitivist" representations of indestructible women to related visions of women by Faulkner and Hemingway. She centers upon Ma Joad and Rose of Sharon and concludes that change and disaster, in Steinbeck, is far better endured by his women than his men.

Introduction

It is eighteen years since John Steinbeck died, and while his popularity as a novelist still endures, his critical reputation has suffered a considerable decline. His honors were many and varied, and included the Nobel Prize and the United States Medal of Freedom. His best novels came early in his career: *In Dubious Battle* (1936); *Of Mice and Men* (1937); *The Grapes of Wrath* (1939). Nothing after that, including *East of Eden* (1952), bears rereading. It would be good to record that rereading his three major novels is a valuable experience, from an aesthetic as well as an historical perspective.

Of Mice and Men, an economical work, really a novella, retains considerable power, marred by an intense sentimentality. But *In Dubious Battle* is now quite certainly a period piece, and is of more interest to social historians than to literary critics. *The Grapes of Wrath,* still Steinbeck's most famous and popular novel, is a very problematical work, and very difficult to judge. As story, or rather, chronicle, it lacks invention, and its characters are not persuasive representations of human inwardness. The book's wavering strength is located elsewhere, in a curious American transformation of biblical substance and style that worked splendidly in Whitman and Hemingway, but seems to work only fitfully in Steinbeck.

Steinbeck suffers from too close a comparison with Hemingway, his authentic precursor though born only three years before his follower. I think that Steinbeck's aesthetic problem *was* Hemingway, whose shadow always hovered too near. Consider the opening of *The Grapes of Wrath:*

> To the red country and part of the gray country of Oklahoma, the last rains came gently, and they did not cut the scarred earth. The plows crossed and recrossed the rivulet marks. The last rains lifted the corn quickly and scattered weed colonies and grass along the sides of the roads so that the gray country and the dark red country began to disappear under a green cover. In

1

the last part of May the sky grew pale and the clouds that had hung in high puffs for so long in the spring were dissipated. The sun flared down on the growing corn day after day until a line of brown spread along the edge of each green bayonet. The clouds appeared, and went away, and in a while they did not try any more. The weeds grew darker green to protect themselves, and they did not spread any more. The surface of the earth crusted, a thin hard crust, and as the sky became pale, so the earth became pale, pink in the red country and white in the gray country.

In the water-cut gullies the earth dusted down in dry little streams. Gophers and ant lions started small avalanches. And as the sharp sun struck day after day, the leaves of the young corn became less stiff and erect; they bent in a curve at first, and then, as the central ribs of strength grew weak, each leaf tilted downward. Then it was June, and the sun shone more fiercely. The brown lines on the corn leaves widened and moved in on the central ribs. The weeds frayed and edged back toward their roots. The air was thin and the sky more pale; and every day the earth paled.

This is not so much biblical style as mediated by Ernest Hemingway, as it is Hemingway assimilated to Steinbeck's sense of biblical style. The monosyllabic diction is hardly the mode of the King James Version, but certainly is Hemingway's. I give, very nearly at random, passages from *The Sun Also Rises:*

We passed through a town and stopped in front of the posada, and the driver took on several packages. Then we started on again, and outside the town the road commenced to mount. We were going through farming country with rocky hills that sloped down into the fields. The grain-fields went up the hillsides. Now as we went higher there was a wind blowing the grain. The road was white and dusty, and the dust rose under the wheels and hung in the air behind us. The road climbed up into the hills and left the rich grain-fields below. Now there were only patches of grain on the bare hillsides and on each side of the water-courses. We turned sharply out to the side of the road to give room to pass to a long string of six mules, following one after the other, hauling a high-hooded wagon loaded with freight. The wagon and the mules were covered with dust. Close behind was another string of mules and another wagon. This was loaded with lumber, and the arriero driving the mules leaned back and put on the thick wooden brakes as we passed. Up here the country was quite barren and the hills were rocky and hard-baked clay furrowed by the rain.

The bus climbed steadily up the road. The country was barren and rocks stuck up through the clay. There was no grass beside the road. Looking back we could see the country spread out below. Far back the fields were squares of green and brown on the hillsides. Making the horizon were the brown mountains. They were strangely shaped. As we climbed higher the horizon kept changing. As the bus ground slowly up the road we could see other mountains coming up in the south. Then the road came over the crest, flattened out, and went into a forest. It was a forest of cork oaks, and the sun came through the trees in patches, and there were cattle grazing back in the trees. We went through the forest and the road came out and turned along a rise of land, and out ahead of us was a rolling green plain, with dark mountains beyond it. These were not like the brown, heat-baked mountains we had left behind. These were wooded and there were clouds coming down from them. The green plain stretched off. It was cut by fences and the white of the road showed through the trunks of a double line of trees that crossed the plain toward the north. As we came to the edge of the rise we saw the red roofs and white houses of Burguete ahead strung out on the plain, and away off on the shoulder of the first dark mountain was the gray metal-sheathed roof of the monastery of Roncevalles.

Hemingway's Basque landscapes are described with an apparent literalness and in what seems at first a curiously dry tone, almost flat in its evident lack of significant emotion. But a closer reading suggests that the style here is itself a metaphor for a passion and a nostalgia that is both defensive and meticulous. The contrast between rich soil and barren ground, between wooded hills and heat-baked mountains, is a figure for the lost potency of Jake Barnes, but also for a larger sense of the lost possibilities of life. Steinbeck, following after Hemingway, cannot learn the lesson. He gives us a vision of the Oklahoma Dust Bowl, and it is effective enough, but it is merely a landscape where a process of entropy has been enacted. It has a social and economic meaning, but as a vision of loss lacks spiritual and personal intensity. Steinbeck is more overtly biblical than Hemingway, but too obviously so. We feel that the Bible's sense of meaning in landscape has returned from the dead in Hemingway's own colors, but hardly in Steinbeck's.

If Steinbeck is not an original or even an adequate stylist, if he lacks skill in plot, and power in the mimesis of character, what then remains in his work, except its fairly constant popularity with an immense number of liberal middlebrows, both in his own country and abroad? Certainly, he aspired beyond his aesthetic means. If the literary Sublime, or contest for the highest place, involves persuading the reader to yield up easier pleasures for more difficult pleasures, and it does, then Steinbeck modestly should have avoided Emerson's American Sublime, but he did not. Desiring it both ways, he fell into bathos in everything he wrote, even in *Of Mice and Men* and *The Grapes of Wrath*.

Yet Steinbeck had many of the legitimate impulses of the Sublime writer, and of his precursors Whitman and Hemingway in particular. Like them, he studied the nostalgias, the aboriginal sources that were never available for Americans, and like them he retained a profound hope for the American as natural man and natural woman. Unlike Whitman and Hemingway and the origin of this American tradition, Emerson, Steinbeck had no capacity for the nuances of literary irony. He had read Emerson's essay "The Over-Soul" as his precursors had, but Steinbeck literalized it. Emerson, canniest where he is most the Idealist, barbs his doctrine of "that Unity, that Over-soul, within which every man's particular being is contained and made one with all other." In Emerson, that does not involve the sacrifice of particular being, and is hardly a program for social action:

> We live in succession, in division, in parts, in particles. Meantime within man is the soul of the whole. . . .
> The soul knows only the soul; all else is idle weeds for her wearing.

There always have been Emersonians of the Left, like Whitman and Steinbeck, and Emersonians of the Right, like Henry James and Wallace Stevens. Emerson himself, rather gingerly planted on the moderate Left, evaded all positions. Social action is also an affair of succession, division, parts, particles; if "the soul knows only the soul," then the soul cannot know doctrines, or even human suffering. Steinbeck, socially generous, a writer on the left, structured the doctrine of *The Grapes of Wrath* on Jim Casy's literalization of Emerson's vision: "Maybe all men got one big soul and everybody's a part of it." Casy, invested by Steinbeck with a rough eloquence that would have moved Emerson, speaks his orator's epitaph just before he is martyred: "They figger I'm a leader 'cause I talk so much." He is a leader, an Okie Moses, and he dies a fitting death for the visionary of an Exodus.

I remain uneasy about my own experience of rereading *The Grapes of Wrath*. Steinbeck is not one of the inescapable American novelists of our century; he cannot be judged in close relation to Cather, Dreiser, and Faulkner, Hemingway and Fitzgerald, Nathanael West, Ralph Ellison, and Thomas Pynchon. Yet there are no canonical standards worthy of human respect that could exclude *The Grapes of Wrath* from a serious reader's esteem. Compassionate narrative that addresses itself so directly to the great social questions of its era is simply too substantial a human achievement to be dismissed. Whether a human strength, however generously worked through, is also an aesthetic value, in a literary narrative, is one of those larger issues that literary criticism scarcely knows how to decide. One might desire *The Grapes of Wrath* to be composed differently, whether as plot or as characterization, but wisdom compels one to be grateful for the novel's continued existence.

The Philosophical Joads

Frederic I. Carpenter

A popular heresy has it that a novelist should not discuss ideas—especially not abstract ideas. Even the best contemporary reviewers concern themselves with the entertainment value of a book (will it please their readers?), and with the impression of immediate reality which it creates. *The Grapes of Wrath,* for instance, was praised for its swift action and for the moving sincerity of its characters. But its mystical ideas and the moralizing interpretations intruded by the author between the narrative chapters were condemned. Presumably the book became a best-seller in spite of these; its art was great enough to overcome its philosophy.

But in the course of time a book is also judged by other standards. Aristotle once argued that poetry should be more "philosophical" than history; and all books are eventually weighed for their content of wisdom. Novels that have become classics do more than tell a story and describe characters; they offer insight into men's motives and point to the springs of action. Together with the moving picture, they offer the criticism of life.

Although this theory of art may seem classical, all important modern novels—especially American novels—have clearly suggested an abstract idea of life. *The Scarlet Letter* symbolized "sin," *Moby-Dick* offered an allegory of evil. *Huck Finn* described the revolt of the "natural individual" against "civilization," and *Babbitt* (like Emerson's "Self-Reliance") denounced the narrow conventions of "society." Now *The Grapes of Wrath* goes beyond these to preach a positive philosophy of life and to damn the blind conservatism which fears ideas.

From *College English* 2, no. 4 (January 1941). © 1941 by the National Council of Teachers of English.

I shall take for granted the narrative power of the book and the vivid reality of its characters: modern critics, both professional and popular, have borne witness to these. The novel is a best-seller. But is also has ideas. These appear abstractly and obviously in the interpretative interchapters. But more important is Steinbeck's creation of Jim Casy, "the preacher," to interpret and to embody the philosophy of the novel. And consummate is the skill with which Jim Casy's philosophy has been integrated with the action of the story, until it motivates and gives significance to the lives of Tom Joad, and Ma, and Rose of Sharon. It is not too much to say that Jim Casy's ideas determine and direct the Joads' actions.

Beside and beyond their function in the story, the ideas of John Steinbeck and Jim Casy possess a significance of their own. They continue, develop, integrate, and realize the thought of the great writers of American history. Here the mystical transcendentalism of Emerson reappears, and the earthy democracy of Whitman, and the pragmatic instrumentalism of William James and John Dewey. And these old philosophies grow and change in the book until they become new. They coalesce into an organic whole. And, finally, they find embodiment in character and action, so that they seem no longer ideas, but facts. The enduring greatness of *The Grapes of Wrath* consists in its imaginative realization of these old ideas in new and concrete forms. Jim Casy translates American philosophy into words of one syllable, and the Joads translate it into action.

II

"Ever know a guy that said big words like that?" asks the truck driver in the first narrative chapter of *The Grapes of Wrath*. "Preacher," replies Tom Joad. "Well, it makes you mad to hear a guy use big words. Course with a preacher it's all right because nobody would fool around with a preacher anyway." But soon afterward Tom meets Jim Casy and finds him changed. "I was a preacher," said the man seriously, "but not no more." Because Casy has ceased to be an orthodox minister and no longer uses big words, Tom Joad plays around with him. And the story results.

But although he is no longer a minister, Jim Casy continues to preach. His words have become simple and his ideas unorthodox. "Just Jim Casy now. Ain't got the call no more. Got a lot of sinful idears—but they seem kinda sensible." A century before, this same experience and essentially these same ideas had occurred to another preacher: Ralph Waldo Emerson had given up the ministry because of his unorthodoxy. But Emerson had kept on using big words. Now Casy translates them: "Why do we got to hang it on God or Jesus? Maybe it's all men an' all women we love; maybe that's the Holy Sperit—the human sperit—the whole shebang. Maybe all men got one big soul ever'body's a apart of." And so the Emersonian oversoul comes to earth in Oklahoma.

Unorthodox Jim Casy went into the Oklahoma wilderness to save his soul. And in the wilderness he experienced the religious feeling of identity with nature which has always been the heart of transcendental mysticism: "There was the hills, an' there was me, an' we wasn't separate no more. We was one thing. An' that one thing was holy." Like Emerson, Casy came to the conviction that holiness, or goodness, results from this feeling of unity: "I got to thinkin' how we was holy when we was one thing, an' mankin' was holy when it was one thing."

Thus far Jim Casy's transcendentalism has remained vague and apparently insignificant. But the corollary of this mystical philosophy is that any man's self-seeking destroys the unity or "holiness" of nature: "An' it [this one thing] on'y got unholy when one mis'able little fella got the bit in his teeth, an' run off his own way. . . . Fella like that bust the holiness." Or, as Emerson phrased it, while discussing Nature: "The world lacks unity because man is disunited with himself. . . . Love is its demand." So Jim Casy preaches the religion of love.

He finds that this transcendental religion alters the old standards: "Here's me that used to give all my fight against the devil 'cause I figured the devil was the enemy. But they's somepin worse'n the devil got hold a the country." Now, like Emerson, he almost welcomes "the dear old devil." Now he fears not the lusts of the flesh but rather the lusts of the spirit. For the abstract lust of possession isolates a man from his fellows and destroys the unity of nature and the love of man. As Steinbeck writes: "The quality of owning freezes you forever into 'I,' and cuts you off forever from the 'we.'" Or, as the Concord farmers in Emerson's poem "Hamatreya" had exclaimed: "'Tis mine, my children's and my name's," only to have "their avarice cooled like lust in the chill of the grave." To a preacher of the oversoul, possessive egotism may become the unpardonable sin.

If a society has adopted "the quality of owning" (as typified by absentee ownership) as its social norm, then Protestant nonconformity may become the highest virtue, and even resistance to authority may become justified. At the beginning of his novel Steinbeck had suggested this, describing how "the faces of the watching men lost their bemused perplexity and became hard and angry and resistant. Then the women knew that they were safe . . . their men were whole." For this is the paradox of Protestantism: when men resist unjust and selfish authority, they themselves become "whole" in spirit.

But this American ideal of nonconformity seems negative: how can men be sure that their Protestant rebellion does not come from the devil? To this there has always been but one answer—faith: faith in the instincts of the common man, faith in ultimate social progress, and faith in the direction in which democracy is moving. So Ma Joad counsels the discouraged Tom: "Why, Tom, we're the people that live. They ain't gonna wipe us out. Why, we're the people—we go on." And so Steinbeck himself affirms a final faith in progress: "When theories change and crash, when schools, philosophies . . . grow and disintegrate, man reaches, stumbles forward. . . . Having stepped forward, he may slip back, but only half a step, never the full step back." Whether this be democratic faith, or mere transcendental optimism, it has always been the motive force of our American life and finds reaffirmation in this novel.

III

Upon the foundation of this old American idealism Steinbeck has built. But the Emersonian oversoul had seemed very vague and very ineffective—only the individual had been real, and he had been concerned more with his private soul than with other people. *The Grapes of Wrath* develops the old idea in new ways. It traces the transformation of the Protestant individual into the member of a social group—the old "I" becomes "we." And it traces the transformation of the passive individual into the active participant—the idealist becomes pragmatist. The first development continues the poetic thought of Walt Whitman; the second continues the philosophy of William James and John Dewey.

"One's-self I sing, a simple separate person," Whitman had proclaimed. "Yet utter the word Democratic, the word En-Masse." Other American writers had emphasized the individual above the group. Even Whitman celebrated his "comrades and lovers" in an essentially personal relationship. But Steinbeck now emphasizes the group above the individual and from an impersonal point of view. Where formerly American and Protestant thought has been separatist, Steinbeck now faces the problem of social integration. In his novel the "mutually repellent particles" of individualism begin to cohere.

"This is the beginning," he writes, "from 'I' to 'we.' " This is the beginning, that is, of reconstruction. When the old society has been split and the Protestant individuals wander aimlessly about, some new nucleus must be found, or chaos and nihilism will follow. "In the night one family camps in a ditch and another family pulls in and the tents come out. The two men squat on their hams and the women and children listen. Here is the node." Here is the new nucleus. "And from this first 'we,' there grows a still more dangerous thing:" 'I have a little food' plus 'I have none.' If from this problem the sum is 'We have a little food,' the thing is on its way, the movement has direction." A new social group is forming, based on the word "en masse." But here is no socialism imposed from above; here is a natural grouping of simple separate persons.

By virtue of his wholehearted participation in this new group the individual may become greater than himself. Some men, of course, will remain mere individuals, but in every group there must be leaders, or "representative men." A poet gives expression to the group idea, or a preacher organizes it. After Jim Casy's death, Tom is chosen to lead. Ma explains: "They's some folks that's just theirself, an' nothin' more. There's Al [for instance] he's jus' a young fella after a girl. You wasn't never like that, Tom." Because he has been an individualist, but through the influence of Casy and of his group idea has become more than himself, Tom becomes "a leader of the people." But his strength derives from his increased sense of participation in the group.

From Jim Casy, and eventually from the thought of Americans like Whitman, Tom Joad has inherited this idea. At the end of the book he sums it up, recalling how Casy "went out in the wilderness to find his own soul, and he found he didn't have no soul that was his'n. Says he foun' he jus' got a little piece of a great big soul. Says a wilderness ain't no good 'cause his little piece of a soul wasn't no good 'less it was with the rest, an' was whole." Unlike Emerson, who had said goodbye to the proud world, these latter-day Americans must live in the midst of it. "I know now," concludes Tom, "a fella ain't no good alone."

To repeat: this group idea is American, not Russian; and stems from Walt Whitman, not Karl Marx. But it does include some elements that have usually seemed sinful to orthodox Anglo-Saxons. "Of physiology from top to toe I sing," Whitman had declared, and added a good many details that his friend Emerson thought unnecessary. Now the Joads frankly discuss anatomical details and joke about them. Like most common people, they do not abscond or conceal. Sometimes they seem to go beyond the bounds of literary decency: the unbuttoned antics of Grandpa Joad touch a new low in folk-comedy. The movies (which reproduced most of the realism of the book) could not quite stomach this. But for the most part they preserved the spirit of the book, because it was whole and healthy.

In Whitman's time almost everyone deprecated this physiological realism, and in our own many readers and critics still deprecate it. Nevertheless, it is absolutely necessary—both artistically and logically. In the first place, characters like the Joads do act and talk that way—to describe them as genteel would be to distort the picture. And, in the second place, Whitman himself had suggested the necessity of it: just as the literature of democracy must describe all sorts of people, "en masse," so it must describe all of the life of the people. To exclude the common or "low" elements of individual life would be as false as to exclude the common or low elements of society. Either would destroy the wholeness of life and nature. Therefore, along with the dust-driven Joads, we must have Grandpa's dirty drawers.

But beyond this physiological realism lies the problem of sex. And this problem is not one of realism at all. Throughout this turbulent novel an almost traditional reticence concerning the details of sex is observed. The problem here is rather one of fundamental morality, for sex had always been a symbol of sin. *The Scarlet Letter* reasserted the authority of an orthodox morality. Now Jim Casy questions that orthodoxy. On this first meeting with Tom he describes how, after sessions of preaching, he had often lain with a girl and then felt sinful afterward. This time the movies repeated his confession, because it is central to the motivation of the story. Disbelief in the sinfulness of sex converts Jim Casy from a preacher of the old morality to a practitioner of the new.

But in questioning the old morality Jim Casy does not deny morality. He doubts the strict justice of Hawthorne's code: "Maybe it ain't a sin. Maybe it's just the way folks is. Maybe we been whippin' the hell out of ourselves for nothin'." But he recognizes that love must always remain responsible and purposeful. Al Joad remains just "a boy after a girl." In place of the old, Casy preaches the new morality of Whitman, which uses sex to symbolize the love of man for his fellows. Jim Casy and Tom Joad have become more responsible and more purposeful than Pa Joad and Uncle John ever were: they love people so much that they are ready to die for them. Formerly the only unit of human love was the family, and the family remains the fundamental unit. The tragedy of *The Grapes of Wrath* consists in the breakup of the family. But the new moral of this novel is that the love of all people—if it be unselfish—may even supersede the love of family. So Casy dies for his people, and Tom is ready to, and Rose of Sharon symbolically transmutes her maternal love to a love of all people. Here is a new realization of "the word democratic, the word en-masse."

IV

"An' I got to thinkin', Ma—most of the preachin' is about the poor we shall have always with us, an' if you got nothin', why, jus' fol' your hands an' to hell with it, you gonna git ice cream on gol' plates when you're dead. An' then this here Preacher says two get a better reward for their work."

Catholic Christianity had always preached humility and passive obedience. Protestantism preached spiritual nonconformity, but kept its disobedience passive. Transcendentalism sought to save the individual but not the group. ("Are they *my* poor?" asked Emerson.) Whitman sympathized more deeply with the common people and loved them abstractly, but trusted that God and democracy would save them. The pragmatic philosophers first sought to implement American idealism by making thought itself instrumental. And now Steinbeck quotes scripture to urge popular action for the realization of the old ideals.

In the course of the book Steinbeck develops and translates the thought of the earlier pragmatists. "Thinking," wrote John Dewey, "is a kind of activity which we perform at specific need." And Steinbeck repeats: "Need is the stimulus to concept, concept to action." The cause of the Okie's migration is their need, and their migration itself becomes a kind of thinking—an unconscious groping for the solution to a half-formulated problem. Their need becomes the stimulus to concept.

In this novel a kind of pragmatic thinking takes place before our eyes: the idea develops from the predicament of the characters, and the resulting action becomes integral with the thought. The evils of absentee ownership produce the mass migration, and the mass migration results in the idea of group action: "A half-million people moving over the country. . . . And tractors turning the multiple furrows in the vacant land."

But what good is generalized thought? And how is future action to be planned? Americans in general, and pragmatists in particular, have always disagreed in answering these questions. William James argued that thought was good only in so far as it satisfied a particular need and that plans, like actions, were "plural"—and should be conceived and executed individually. But Charles Sanders Peirce, and the transcendentalists before him, had argued that the most generalized thought was best, provided it eventually resulted in effective action. The problems of mankind should be considered as a unified whole, monistically.

Now Tom Joad is a pluralist—a pragmatist after William James. Tom said, "I'm still layin' my dogs down one at a time." Casy replied: "Yeah, but when a fence comes up at ya, ya gonna climb that fence." "I climb fences when I got fences to climb," said Tom. But Jim Casy believes in looking far ahead and seeing the thing as a whole: "But they's different kinda fences. They's folks like me that climbs fences that ain't even strang up yet." Which is to say that Casy is a kind of transcendental pragmatist. His thought seeks to generalize the problems of the Okies and to integrate them with the larger problem of industrial America. His solution is the principle of group action guided by conceptual thought and functioning within the framework of democratic society and law.

And at the end of the story Tom Joad becomes converted to Jim Casy's pragmatism. It is not important that the particular strike should be won, or that the particular need should be satisfied; but it is important that men should think in terms of action, and that they should think and act in terms of the whole rather than the particular individual. "For every little beaten strike is proof that the step is being taken." The value of an idea lies not in its immediate but in its eventual success. That idea is good which works— in the long run.

But the point of the whole novel is that action is an absolute essential of human life. If need and failure produce only fear, disintegration follows. But if they produce anger, then reconstruction may follow. The grapes of wrath must be trampled to make manifest the glory of the Lord. At the beginning of the story Steinbeck described the incipient wrath of the defeated farmers. At the end he repeats the scene. "And where a number of men gathered together, the fear went from their faces, and anger took its place. And the women sighed with relief . . . the break would never come as long as fear could turn to wrath." Then wrath could turn to action.

V

To sum up: the fundamental idea of The Grapes of Wrath is that of American transcendentalism: "Maybe all men got one big soul every'body's a part of." From this idea it follows that every individual will trust those instincts which he shares with all men, even when these conflict with the teachings of orthodox religion and of existing society. But his self-reliance will not merely seek individual freedom, as did Emerson. It will rather seek social freedom or mass democracy, as did Whitman. If this mass democracy leads to the abandonment of genteel taboos and to the modification of some traditional ideas of morality, that is inevitable. But whatever happens, the American will act to realize his ideals. He will seek to make himself whole— i.e., to join himself to other men by means of purposeful actions for some goal beyond himself.

But at this point the crucial question arises—and it is "crucial" in every sense of the word. What if this self-reliance lead to death? What if the individual is killed before the social group is saved? Does the failure of the individual action invalidate the whole idea? "How'm I gonna know about you?" Ma asks. "They might kill ya an' I wouldn't know."

The answer has already been suggested by the terms in which the story has been told. If the individual has identified himself with the oversoul, so that his life has become one with the life of all men, his individual death and failure will not matter. From the old transcendental philosophy of identity to Tom Joad and the moving pictures may seem a long way, but even the movies faithfully reproduced Tom's final declaration of transcendental faith: "They might kill ya," Ma had objected.

> Tom laughed uneasily, "Well, maybe like Casy says, a fella ain't got a soul of his own, but on'y a piece of a big one—an' then—"
>
> "Then what, Tom?"
>
> "Then it don' matter. Then I'll be aroun' in the dark. I'll be ever'where—wherever you look. Wherever they's a fight so hungry people can eat, I'll be there. Wherever they's a cop beating up a guy, I'll be there. If Casy knowed, why, I'll be in the way guys yell when they're mad, an'—I'll be in the way kids laugh when they're hungry an' they know supper's ready. An' when our folks eat the stuff they raise an' live in the houses they build—why, I'll be there. See?"

For the first time in history, *The Grapes of Wrath* brings together and makes real three great skeins of American thought. It begins with the transcendental oversoul, Emerson's faith in the common man, and his Protestant self-reliance. To this it joins Whitman's religion of the love of all men and his mass democracy. And it combines these mystical and poetic ideas with the realistic philosophy of pragmatism and its emphasis on effective action. From this it develops a new kind of Christianity—not otherworldly and passive, but earthly and active. And Oklahoma Jim Casy and the Joads think and do all these philosophical things.

The Fully Matured Art:
The Grapes of Wrath

Howard Levant

The enormous contemporary social impact of *The Grapes of Wrath* can encourage the slippery reasoning that condemns a period novel to die with its period. But continuing sales and critical discussions suggest that *The Grapes of Wrath* has outlived its directly reportorial ties to the historical past; that it can be considered as an aesthetic object, a good or a bad novel per se. In that light, the important consideration is the relative harmony of its structure and materials.

The Grapes of Wrath is an attempted prose epic, a summation of national experience at a given time. Evaluation proceeds from that identification of genre. A negative critical trend asserts that *The Grapes of Wrath* is too flawed to command serious attention: the materials are local and temporary, not universal and permanent; the conception of life is overly simple; the characters are superficial types (except, perhaps, Ma Joad); the language is folksy or strained by turns; and, in particular, the incoherent structure is the weakest point—the story breaks in half, the nonorganic, editorializing interchapters force unearned general conclusions, and the ending is inconclusive as well as overwrought and sentimental. The positive trend asserts that *The Grapes of Wrath* is a great novel. Its materials are properly universalized in specific detail; the conception is philosophical, the characters are warmly felt and deeply created; the language is functional, varied, and superb on the whole; and the structure is an almost perfect combination of the dramatic and the panoramic in sufficient harmony with the materials. This criticism

From *The Novels of John Steinbeck: A Critical Study*. © 1974 by the Curators of the University of Missouri. University of Missouri Press, 1974.

admits that overwrought idealistic passages as well as propagandistic simplifications turn up on occasion, but these are minor flaws in an achievement on an extraordinary scale. Relatively detached studies of Steinbeck's ideas comprise a third trend. These studies are not directly useful in analytical criticism; they do establish that Steinbeck's social ideas are ordered and legitimate extensions of biological fact, hence scientific and true rather than mistaken or sentimental.

The two evaluative positions are remarkable in their opposition. They are perhaps overly simple in asserting that *The Grapes of Wrath* is either a classic of our literature or a formless pandering to sentimental popular taste. Certainly these extremes are mistaken in implying (when they do) that, somehow, *The Grapes of Wrath* is sui generis in relation to Steinbeck's work.

Trends so awkwardly triple need to be brought into a sharper focus. By way of a recapitulation in focus, consider a few words of outright praise:

> For all of its sprawling asides and extravagances, *The Grapes of Wrath* is a big book, a great book, and one of maybe two or three American novels in a class with *Huckleberry Finn*.

Freeman Champney's praise is conventional enough to pass unquestioned if one admires *The Grapes of Wrath,* or, if one does not, it can seem an invidious borrowing of prestige, shrilly emotive at that. Afterthought emphasizes the serious qualification of the very high praise. Just how much damage is wrought by those "sprawling asides and extravagances," and does *The Grapes of Wrath* survive its structural faults as *Huckleberry Finn* does, by virtue of its mythology, its characterization, its language? If the answers remain obscure, illumination may increase (permitting, as well, a clearer definition of the aesthetic efficacy of Steinbeck's ideas) when the context of critical discussion is the relationship of the novel's structure to its materials.

Steinbeck's serious intentions and his artistic honesty are not in question. He had studied and experienced the materials intensely over a period of time. After a false start that he rejected (*L'Affaire Lettuceburg*), his conscious intention was to create an important literary work rather than a propagandistic shocker or a journalistic statement of the topical problem of how certain people faced one aspect of the Great Depression. Therefore, it is an insult to Steinbeck's aims to suggest that somehow *The Grapes of Wrath* is imperfect art but a "big" or "great" novel nevertheless. In all critical justice, *The Grapes of Wrath* must stand or fall as a serious and important work of art.

The consciously functional aspect of Steinbeck's intentions—his working of the materials—is clarified by a comparison of *The Grapes of Wrath* with *In Dubious Battle*. Both novels deal with labor problems peculiar to California, but that similarity cannot be pushed too far. The Joads are fruit pickers in California, but not of apples, the fruit mentioned in *In Dubious Battle*. The Joads pick cotton, and in the strike novel the people expect to move on to cotton. The Joads become involved in a strike but as strike-breakers rather than as strikers. Attitudes are less easy to camouflage. The strikers in *In Dubious Battle* and the Okies in *The Grapes of Wrath* are presented with sympathy whereas the owning class and much of the middle class have no saving virtue. The sharpest similarity is that both the strikers and the Okies derive a consciousness of the need for group action from their experiences; but even here there is a difference in emphasis. The conflict of interest is more pointed and the lessons of experience are less ambiguous in *The Grapes of Wrath* than in *In Dubious Battle*. The fact is that the two novels are not similar beyond a common basis in California labor problems, and Steinbeck differentiates that basis carefully in most specific details. The really significant factor is that different structures are appropriate to each novel. The restricted scope of *In Dubious Battle* demands a dramatic structure with some panoramic elements as they are needed. The broad scope of *The Grapes of Wrath* demands a panoramic structure; the dramatic elements appear as they are needed. Therefore, in each case, the primary critical concern must be the adequacy of the use of the materials, not the materials in themselves.

Steinbeck's profound respect for the materials of *The Grapes of Wrath* is recorded in a remarkable letter in which he explained to his literary agents and to his publisher the main reason for his withdrawing *L'Affaire Lettuce-burg*, the hurried, propagandistic, thirty-thousand-word manuscript novel that preceded *The Grapes of Wrath*:

> I know I promised this book to you, and that I am breaking a promise in withholding it. But I had got smart and cagey you see. I had forgotten that I hadn't learned to write books, that I will never learn to write them. A book must be a life that lives all of itself and this one doesn't do that. You can't write a book. It isn't that simple. The process is more painful than that. And this book is fairly clever, has skillful passages, but tricks and jokes. Sometimes I, the writer, seem a hell of a smart guy—just twisting this people out of shape. But the hell with it. I beat poverty for a good many years and I'll be damned if I'll go down at the first little whiff of success. I hope you, Pat, don't think

I've double-crossed you. In the long run to let this book out
would be to double-cross you. But to let the bars down is like
a first theft. It's hard to do, but the second time it isn't so hard
and pretty soon it is easy. If I should write three books like this
and let them out, I would forget there were any other kinds.

This is Steinbeck's declaration of artistic purpose—and his effort to exorcise
a dangerous (and permanent) aspect of his craft. Much of the motivation
for Steinbeck's career is stated in this letter. After all, he did write *L'Affaire
Lettuceburg*; and "tricks and jokes," detached episodes, and detached ironic
hits, as well as a twisting of characters, are evident enough in much of
Steinbeck's earlier work. But the depression materials were too serious to
treat lightly or abstractly, or to subject to an imposed structure (mistaken
idealism, nature worship, a metaphysical curse, a literary parallel). Such
materials need to be in harmony with an appropriate structure.

From that intentional perspective, the central artistic problem is to
present the universal and epical in terms of the individual and particular.
Steinbeck chooses to deal with this by creating an individual, particular
image of the epical experience of the dispossessed Okies by focusing a
sustained attention on the experience of the Joads. The result is an organic
combination of structures. Dramatic structure suits the family's particular
history; panoramic structure proves out the representative nature of their
history. To avoid a forced and artificial "typing," to assure that extensions
of particular detail are genuinely organic, Steinbeck postulates a conceptual
theme that orders structure and materials: the transformation of the Joad
family from a self-contained, self-sustaining unit to a conscious part of a
group, a whole larger than its parts. This thematic ordering is not merely
implicit or ironic, as it is in *The Pastures of Heaven,* or withheld to create
mystery as in *Cup of Gold* or *To a God Unknown*. Steinbeck chances the
strength of the materials and the organic quality of their structure. And he
defines differences: the group is not group-man. The earlier concept is a
"beast," created by raw emotion ("blood"), short-lived, unwieldly, un-
predictable, mindless; a monster that produces indiscriminate good or evil.
The group is quite different—rational, stable, relatively calm—because it is
an assemblage of like-minded people who retain their individual and traditional sense of right and wrong as a natural fact. Group-man lacks a moral
dimension; the group is a morally pure instrument of power. The difference
is acute at the level of leadership. The leaders have ambiguous aims in *In
Dubious Battle,* but they are Christ-like (Jim Casy) or attain moral insight
(Tom Joad) in *The Grapes of Wrath*.

The Grapes of Wrath is optimistic; *In Dubious Battle* is not. That the living part of the Joad family survives, though on the edge of survival, is less than glowingly optimistic, but that survival produces a mood that differs considerably from the unrelenting misery of *In Dubious Battle*. Optimism stems from the theme, most openly in the alternation of narrative chapter and editorial interchapter. While the Joads move slowly and painfully toward acceptance of the group, many of the interchapters define the broad necessity of that acceptance. Arbitrary plotting does not produce this change. Its development is localized in Ma Joad's intense focus on the family's desire to remain a unit; her recognition of the group is the dramatic resolution. ("Use' ta be the fambly was fust. It ain't so now. It's anybody. Worse off we get, the more we got to do.") Optimism is demonstrated also in experience that toughens, educates, and enlarges the stronger Joads in a natural process. On the simplest, crudest level, the family's journey and ordeal is a circumstantial narrative of an effort to reach for the good material life. Yet that is not the sole motive, and those members who have only that motive leave the family. On a deeper level, the family is attempting to rediscover the identity it lost when it was dispossessed; so the Joads travel from order (their old, traditional life) through disorder (the road, California) to some hope of a better, rediscovered order, which they reach in Ma's recognition and Tom's dedication. Their journey toward order is the ultimate optimistic, ennobling process, the earned, thematic resolution of the novel.

I do not intend to imply that Steinbeck pretties his materials. He does not stint the details of the family's various privations, its continual losses of dignity, and the death or disappearance of many of its members. On the larger scale, there is considerable objective documentation of the general economic causes of such misery—a circumstantial process that lifts *The Grapes of Wrath* out of the merely historic genre of the proletarian novel. Optimism survives as the ultimate value because of the will of the people to understand and to control the conditions of their lives despite constant discouragement.

This value is essentially abstract, political. Steinbeck deepens and universalizes it by developing the relationship between the family unit and "the people." The family is made up of unique individuals. "The people" embraces a timeless entity, a continuing past, present, and future of collective memory—but free of any social or political function. Time lag confounds the usefulness of "the people" as a guide for the present. The Joads and others like them know they may keep the land or get new land if they can kill or control "the Bank," as the old people killed Indians to take the land and controlled nature to keep it. But "the Bank" is more complicated an enemy than Indians or nature because it is an abstraction. (That buccaneering capitalism is an abstract or allegorical monster of evil is left to implication in *In Dubious Battle*. Steinbeck is far more directly allegorical in characterizing "the Bank" as an evil, nonhuman monster. Consequently there is, I think, a gain in horror but a relative loss of credibility.) So the Okies submit to dispossession in Oklahoma (forced by mechanized cheaper production of cotton) and to the huge migration into California (encouraged by landowners to get cheap field labor), motivated by the time lag that confuses them, for none of them comprehends the monstrous logic of modern economics. Despite their ignorance, in a process that is unifying in itself and is second only to survival, the families work at some way of prevailing against "the Bank." The older, agrarian concept of "the people" is succeeded in time by the new concept of the group, an instrument of technology and political power—an analogue that works. Steinbeck makes this succession appear necessary and legitimate by a representation that excludes alternate solutions. The permitted solution seems a natural evolution, from people to group, because it is a tactic, not a fundamental change in folkways. Its process is long and painful because the emotive entity, "the people," needs to feel its way toward redefinition as the group—the abstract, political entity which emerges as an organic, particularized whole. This is brilliant literary strategy, in its grasp of operative metaphor and its avoidance of an overly obvious, loaded opposition. Steinbeck is scrupulously careful to keep to precise and exact circumstantial detail in this developed metaphor. Concretely, the panicky violence of "the Bank" is the reverse of the fact that (seemingly by habit) the Joads are kind to those who need their help and neighborly to people who are like them. The metaphor is persuasive.

Steinbeck is quite as scrupulous in the use of allegory as a way of universalizing an abstract particular. In his earlier work this method can produce a tangibly artificial, forced result, but allegory is a credible and functional device in *The Grapes of Wrath.* The turtle episode in chapter 3 is justly famous. Objectively, we have a fully realized description of a land turtle's patient, difficult journey over dust fields, across a road and walled embankment, and on through the dust. The facts are the starting point; nature is not distorted or manipulated to yield allegorical meaning. The turtle seems awkward but it is able to survive, like the Joads, and like them it is moving southwest, out of the dry area. It can protect itself against a natural danger like the red ant it kills, as the Joads protect themselves by their unity. The turtle's eyes are "fierce, humorous," suggesting force that takes itself easily; the stronger Joads are a fierce, humorous people. When mismanaged human power attacks, as when a truck swerves to hit the turtle, luck is on the animal's side—it survives by luck. The Joads survive the mismanagement that produced the Dust Bowl and the brutalizing man-made conditions in California as much by luck as by design. The relation to the Joads of the life-bearing function of the turtle is more obscure, or perhaps overly ambitious. The factual starting point is that, unknowingly, the turtle carries an oat seed in its shell and unknowingly drops and plants the seed in the dust, where it will rest until water returns. The most obvious link in the Joad family is the pregnant Rose of Sharon, but her baby is born dead. Perhaps compassion is "born," as in Uncle John's thoughts as he floats the dead baby down the flooding river in its apple box coffin: "Go down an' tell 'em. Go down in the street an' rot an' tell 'em that way. That's the way you can talk. . . . Maybe they'll know then." (The reversal of values is evident in the reversed symbolism; the river bears death—not life, the coffin—not water to seeds in the earth.) But this appeal is strained, too greatly distanced from the factual starting point. The link works in the restricted sense that Ruthie and Winfield are "planted," and will perhaps take root, in the new environment of California. At this point the careful allegory collapses under its own weight, yet care is taken to join the device to the central narrative. In chapter 4, Tom Joad picks up a turtle, and later Casy remarks on the tenacity of the breed:

> "Nobody can't keep a turtle though. They work at it and work at it, and at last one day they get out and away they go— off somewheres."

This recognition of the turtle's purposeful tenacity interprets and places the preceding interchapter in the central narrative. Tom calls the turtle "an old bulldozer," a figure that works in opposition to the threatening insect life the tractors suggest as self-defeating, destructive tools of "the Bank." Again, a purposeful turtle is opposed to homeless domestic animals, like the "thick-furred yellow shepherd dog" that passes Tom and Casy, to suggest precisely the ruined land and the destruction of the old ways of life on the most basic, animal level, where the wild (or free) animal survives best. These and other supporting details extend the exemplum into the narrative; they continue and deepen Steinbeck's foreshadowing, moralizing insight naturally, within the range of biological imagery. It is true, allowing for the one collapse of the allegory, that none of Steinbeck's earlier work exhibits as profound a comprehension of what can be done to "place" an allegorical narrative device.

The turtle interchapter is masterful enough. Steinbeck does even more with an extended instance of allegorizing—the introduction of the lapsed preacher, Jim Casy, into the Joad family. Casy has a role that is difficult to present within the limits of credibility. Casy may look too much like his function, the Christ-like force that impels the family toward its transformation into the group. If the novel is to have more significance than a reportorial narrative of travel and hardship, Casy's spiritual insights are a necessary means of stating a convincing philosophical optimism. The technical difficulty is that Casy does not have a forthright narrative function. He drops out of the narrative for almost one hundred and fifty pages, although his presence continues through the Joads' wondering at times what had happened to him. When he reenters the novel, he is killed off within fifteen pages—sacrificed for the group in accord with his Christ-like function, with a phrase that recalls Christ's last words. In spite of the obvious technical difficulty in handling such materials, Steinbeck realizes Casy as fully as any of the major Joads. Casy's struggle with himself to define "sin" to include the necessary facts of the natural world lends him a completely human aspect. He earns the right to make moral statements because he bases all judgments on his own experience. This earned right to "witness" serves to keep Casy human, yet it permits him to function as if he were an allegorical figure. This is a brilliant solution, and Casy is Steinbeck's most successful use of a functional allegorical figure in a major role. His narrative sharpness contrasts amazingly with the dim realization of Sir Henry Morgan or Joseph Wayne.

Even Casy's necessary distance is functional rather than arbitrary. He exists outside the narrative in the sense that he travels with the Joads but he is not a member of the family, and there is no danger of confusing his adventures with theirs. Further, by right of his nature and experience, he has the function of being the living moral conscience of "the people." He travels with the Joads to witness the ordeal of the Okies, to understand its causes, and to do what he can to help. Steinbeck's convincing final touch is that, at the end, Tom Joad aspires to Casy's role. In this shift, Steinbeck manipulates allegory, he does not submit to its rigid quality, for Tom is not like Casy. Tom is far more violent, more capable of anger; having been shown the way, however, he may be more successful as a practical missionary than Casy. One might say that if Casy is to be identified with Christ, the almost human god, Tom is to be identified with Saint Paul, the realistic, tough organizer. The allegorical link by which Tom is "converted" and assumes Casy's role is deeply realized and rich with significance, not simply because it is a technical necessity, but because it is a confirmation of Casy's reality as a man and a teacher. The parallels to Christ and Saint Paul would be only arid technical facts if they were not realized so profoundly. The trivial fact that Casy has Christ's initials dims beside this more profound and sustained realization.

Function, not mere design, is as evident in the use of characterization to support and develop a conflict of opposed ideas—mainly a struggle between law and anarchy. The one idea postulates justice in a moral world of love and work, identified in the past with "the people" and in the present with the government camp and finally with the union movement, since these are the modern, institutional forms the group may take. The opposed idea postulates injustice in an immoral world of hatred and starvation. It is associated with buccaneering capitalism, which, in violent form, includes strikebreaking and related practices that cheapen human labor.

The Joads present special difficulties in characterization. They must be individualized to be credible and universalized to carry out their representative functions. Steinbeck meets these problems by making each of the Joads a specific individual and by specifying that what happens to the Joads is typical of the times. The means he uses to maintain these identities can be shown in some detail. The least important Joads are given highly specific tags—Grandma's religion, Grandpa's vigor, Uncle John's melancholy, and Al's love of cars and girls. The tags are involved in events; they are not inert labels. Grandma's burial violates her religion; Grandpa's vigor ends when he leaves the land; Uncle John's melancholy balances the family's experience; Al helps to drive the family to California and, by marrying, continues the family. Ma, Pa, Rose of Sharon, and Tom carry the narrative, so their individuality is defined by events rather than through events. Ma is the psychological and moral center of the family; Pa carries its burdens; Rose of Sharon means to ensure its physical continuity; and Tom becomes its moral conscience. On the larger scale, there is much evidence that what happens to the family is typical of the times. The interchapters pile up suggestions that "the whole country is moving" or about to move. The Joads meet many of their counterparts or outsiders who are in sympathy with their ordeal; these meetings reenforce the common bond of "the people." Both in the interchapters and the narrative, the universal, immediate issue is survival—a concrete universal.

On the other hand, the individualized credibility of the Joads is itself the source of two difficulties: the Joads are too different, as sharecroppers, to suggest a universal or even a national woe, and they speak an argot that might limit their universal quality. (It is a curious fact that Steinbeck attempts to create a so-called "universal language" in *Burning Bright,* a far more theory-ridden novel than *The Grapes of Wrath*. In any event, the attempt produces a fantastic, wholly incredible language.) Steinbeck handles these limitations with artistic license. The narrative background contains the Joads' past; their experience as a landless proletariat is highlighted in the narrative foreground. The argot is made to seem a typical language within the novel in three ways: it is the major language; people who are not Okies speak variations of their argot; and that argot is not specialized in its relevance, but is used to communicate the new experiences "the people" have in common as a landless proletariat. However, because these solutions depend on artistic license, any tonal falseness undermines severely the massive artistic truthfulness the language is intended to present. So the overly editorial tone in several of the interchapters has a profoundly false linguistic ring, although the tonal lapse is limited and fairly trivial in itself.

The Joads are characterized further in comparison with four Okie types who refuse to know or are unable to gain the knowledge the family derives from its collective experience. They are the stubborn, the dead, the weak, and the backtrackers; they appear in the novel in that order.

Muley Graves is the stubborn man, as his punning name suggests. He reveals himself to Tom and Casy near the beginning of the novel. His refusal to leave Oklahoma is mere stubbornness; his isolation drives him somewhat mad. He is aware of a loss of reality, of "jus' wanderin' aroun' like a damn ol' graveyard ghos'," and his blind violence is rejected from the beginning by the strongest, who oppose his pessimism with an essential optimism.

Deaths of the aged and the unborn frame the novel. Grandpa and Grandma are torn up by the roots and die, incapable of absorbing a new, terrible experience. Rose of Sharon's baby, born dead at the end of the novel, is an index of the family's ordeal and a somewhat contrived symbol of the necessity to form the group.

The weak include two extremes within the Joad family. Noah Joad gives up the struggle to survive; he finds a private peace. His character is shadowy, and his choice is directed more clearly by Steinbeck than by any substance within him. Connie has plenty of substance. He is married to Rose of Sharon and deserts her because he had no faith in the family's struggle to reach California. His faith is absorbed in the values of "the Bank," in getting on, in money, in any abstract goal. He wishes to learn about technology in order to rise in the world. He does not admire technique for itself, as Al does. He is a sexual performer, but he loves no one. Finally, he wishes that he had stayed behind in Oklahoma and taken a job driving a tractor. In short, with Connie, Steinbeck chooses brilliantly to place a

"Bank" viewpoint within the family. By doing so, he precludes a simplification of character and situation, and he endorses the complexity of real people in the real world. (*In Dubious Battle* is similarly free of schematic characterization.) In addition, the family's tough, humanistic values gain in credibility by their contrast with Connie's shallow, destructive modernity. The confused gas station owner and the pathetic one-eyed junkyard helper are embodied variations on Connie's kind of weakness. Al provides an important counterpoint. He wants to leave the family at last, like Connie, but duty and love force him to stay. His hard choice points the moral survival of the family and measures its human expense.

The Joads meet several backtrackers. The Wilsons go back because Mrs. Wilson is dying; the Joads do not stop, in spite of death. The ragged man's experience foreshadows what the Joads find in California; but they keep on. Some members of the Joad family think of leaving but do not, or they leave for specific reasons—a subtle variation on backtracking. Al and Uncle John wish deeply at times to leave, but they stay; Tom leaves (as Casy does) but to serve the larger, universal family of the group. Backtracking is a metaphor, then, a denial of life, but always a fact as well. The factual metaphor is deepened into complexity because the Joads sympathize with the backtrackers' failure to endure the hardships of the road and of California, in balance with where they started from—the wasteland—while knowing they cannot accept that life-denying solution. All of these choices are the fruit of the family's experience.

A fifth group of owners and middle-class people are accorded no sympathetic comprehension, as contrasted with the Joads, and, as in *In Dubious Battle,* their simply and purely monstrous characterization is too abstract to be fully credible. The few exceptions occur in highly individualized scenes or episodes (chapter 15 is an example) in which middle-class "shitheels" are caricatures of the bad guys, limited to a broad contrast with the good guys (the truck drivers, the cook), who are in sympathy with a family of Okies. (Fifteen years later, Steinbeck detailed this technique in a witty article, "How to Tell Good Guys from Bad Guys," *The Reporter* 12 [March 10, 1955], 42–44. In that quite different, political context, Steinbeck demonstrates that he knows the technique is too bluntly black and white to permit any but the broadest cartoon characterization. There is every reason to think he knew as much in 1935 or 1939.) This limitation has the narrative advantage of highlighting the importance and vitality of the Okies to the extent that they seem by right to belong in the context of epic materials, but the disadvantage of shallow characterization is severe. Steinbeck can provide a convincing detailed background of the conditions of the time; he cannot similarly give a rounded, convincing characterization to an owner or a disagreeable middle-class person.

On the whole, then, fictive strength and conviction are inherent in the materials of *The Grapes of Wrath*. The noticeable flaws are probably irreducible aspects of the time context and of narrative shorthand, counterpointed by a complex recognition of human variety in language and behavior.

The ordering of the structure supports this conclusion. *The Grapes of Wrath* has three parts: Tom's return and his witnessing of events; the family's departure and experiences on the road; its arrival and experiences in California. The interchapters "locate" and generalize the narrative chapters, somewhat like stage directions. They supply, in a suitably dramatic or rhetorical style, information the Joads cannot possess, and they are involved more often than not in the narrative. (Because of that involvement, it is incorrect to think of the interchapters as choral. We see the difference in comparing the four detached interchapters in *Cup of Gold* with any interchapters in *The Grapes of Wrath,* and we see as well Steinbeck's artistic growth in the organic integration of chapter and interchapter in the later novel. The stylistic variety always suited to its content is further evidence of a conscious, intentional artistry.) This device provides for both precise detail and epic scope. The imagery fulfills the structural purpose of pitting life against death.

The first part contains ten chapters. The opening is a "location" interchapter. The dead land of the Dust Bowl in Oklahoma provides the imagery of a universal death, but at the close the women watch their men to see if they will break in the stress of that natural disaster. The men do not break; the scene is repeated in California at the close of the novel in a rising rhetoric. The objective imagistic frame sets life against death, and life endures in the will of the people to endure. The following nine chapters center on Tom's return from a kind of death—prison. With Casy, Tom is an external observer, witnessing with fresh eyes the dead land and the universal dispossession. Death seems to prevail. The turtle interchapter is recapitulated ironically in the narrative. Pa carries handbills that promise jobs in California, an analogue to the turtle carrying a head of oats; but the handbills falsely promise renewal; their intention is to cheapen the labor market. Later events prove the group concept is the genuine renewal, the true goal. Immediately, death is associated with "the Bank," an abstraction presented concretely in symbolic form as the tractor—the perfect tool of the abstract "Bank," which dehumanizes its driver and kills the fertility of the land.

When he sees the abandoned Joad home, Tom says, "Maybe they're all dead," but Muley Graves tells Tom the family is alive, with Uncle John, and about to leave without him for California. Tom is reborn or returned to life within the family, but its vital center has shifted (as represented in charged, frankly mystical terms) to a life-giving machine:

> The family met at the most important place, near the truck. The house was dead, and the fields were dead; but this truck was the active thing, the living principle.

The family's certainties develop from an ironically hopeful innocence, a failure to realize that a new basis for life has overtaken them, replacing family with group. The trek is an instinctive flight from death, but the economic system is more deadly than the drouth. The Joads accept the promise of the handbills, they are cheated when they sell their farm equipment, but they do not doubt that they will transplant themselves in California. The real certainty is the death of the past, as in the burning of relics by an unnamed woman in an interchapter, and by Ma herself, just before the trek begins.

All that is not dead is altered. Pa's loss of authority to Ma and Al's new authority (he knows automobiles) represent the shifts in value within the family. They retain a living coherence as farmers. They work as a unit when they kill and salt down the hogs in preparation for the trek. They are innocent of the disgusting techniques of close dealing in business, but Tom explains to Casy how the Joads can deal closely enough in their accustomed agrarian context. Their innocence, therefore, is touching, not comic, and their literal preparations support a symbolic preparation, a blindly hopeful striving to find life. Their journey is an expression, despite all shocks and changes, of the will to survive; hence, it has an epic dignity, echoing their retained, personal dignity.

In all the imagery of life and death, Steinbeck is consistent in that his symbols grow out of objective, literal facts. He thus achieves imagery in a more fully realized texture in this novel than in earlier work. This organically realized symbolism is maintained and developed in the seven chapters of the second section.

With the dead land behind them, the family carries the death of the past on its journey. Grandpa dies on the first night. Probably his stroke is caused, at least in part, by the "medicine" that Ma and Tom dope him with to take him away from the land—for the good of the family as a whole. An incipient group concept emerges in this overriding concern for the whole. Grandpa's death is offset by the meeting of the Joads and the Wilsons.

At the beginning, Grandpa's illness and death join the two families in bonds of sympathy. There are other unifying forces; the language bar becomes senseless, and the two families help each other. Casy sees the emergence of the group, the whole absorbing the individual, in his sermon for Grandpa:

> Casy said solemnly, "This here ol' man jus' lived a life an' jus' died out of it. I don't know whether he was good or bad, but that don't matter much. He was alive, an' that's what matters. An' now he's dead, an' that don't matter. Heard a fella tell a poem one time, an' he says, 'All that lives is holy.' "

A modest dignity embodies the vitalistic dogma. As a further push from individual to group, the family decides to break the law by burying Grandpa secretly beside the road; a conventional funeral would eat up the money they need to reach California. Grandma's grisly, circumstantial death is delayed until the end of the section; it outweighs the achievement of reaching their destination and foreshadows the reality of California. True, the family can absorb death, even new kinds of death, into its experience. Ruthie and Winfield react most violently to the dog's death at the first stop on the road; they are less affected by Grandpa's death, still less by Grandma's. Late on the night of Grandpa's death after the Joads and Wilsons have agreed to join forces, Ma remarks: "Grandpa—it's like he's dead a year." Experience breeds a calm in the face of loss that fills in the past. Tom points this harshly realistic network of difference after Grandma's death:

> "They was too old," he said. "They wouldn't of saw nothin' that's here. Grampa would a been a-seein' the Injuns an' the prairie country when he was a young fella. An' Granma would a remembered an' seen the first home she lived in. They was too ol'. Who's really seein' it is Ruthie and Winfiel'."

Life matters. The narrative context supports this fruit of the family's private experience. Between the deaths of Grandpa and Grandma, the Joads meet several symbolically dead people on the road. The gas station owner is incapable of learning the meaning of his own experience even when it is explained to him. The one-eyed junkyard helper lives in a prison of self, inside his ugly face and unclean body. Tom (who was in an actual prison) tries unsuccessfully to force him from his death into life. The several returning sharecroppers have come to accept a living death as the only reality. They have cut themselves off from the inchoate struggle to form a group, admittedly against severe odds, so they have no choice but to return to the dead, empty land.

But to outsiders, seeing only the surface, the Joads are not heroic life-bearers but stupidly ignorant, as in a dialogue between two service station boys when the family leaves on the final lap of the trek, the night trip across the Mojave Desert:

> "Jesus, I'd hate to start out in a jalopy like that." "Well, you and me got sense. Them goddamn Okies got no sense and no feeling. They ain't human. A human being wouldn't live like they do. A human being couldn't stand to be so dirty and miserable. They ain't a hell of a lot better than gorillas." "Just the same. I'm glad I ain't crossing the desert in no Hudson Super-Six. . . . " "You know, they don't have much trouble. They're so goddamn dumb they don't know it's dangerous. And, Christ Almighty, they don't know any better than what they got. Why worry?"

The dialogue is exactly true, but the truth is ironic. The Joads do have the appearance of death, and ignorant, dirty, dispossessed yokels seem to be unlikely carriers of an affirmation of life. The ironic truth defines the heroism of the Joads. The family is aware of the dangers of the desert crossing, and Grandma dies during it, "for the fambly," as Ma says. In general the family is more aware than the boys at the service station are allowed to know. After meeting a second returning sharecropper, the Joads are even aware of the actual conditions in California; Uncle John, the family's weakest moral agent, voices the family's rejection of despair when he says, "We're a-goin' there, ain't we? None of this here talk gonna keep us from goin' there." The service station boys express, so we can dismiss, a superficially sentimental view of the Joads. The ironic truth is that the family goes ahead, knowing the dangers and aware that California may not be Eden. Their genuine heroism and nobility are all the more valid for being tested by irony.

Yet there is no suggestion that the Joads are merely deterministic formulae. They are pawns of circumstance up to a point. They react to events they do not understand fully, and no doubt partial ignorance and pure necessity keep them on the road and get them to California. But Ma and Tom undergo certain developments of character that exclude determinism. Ma's constantly increasing moral authority is her response to the forces that are tearing the family apart, but she acts out of love that is restricted to the family, that is not universalized until very near the end of the novel. Tom's role is more extensive and more complex. He begins by regarding himself as a creature of necessity—"I ruther jus'—lay one foot down in front a the other"—but his quietism relates to a prison experience he does not want to live "over an' over." His natural understanding of why and how people behave forces him into a moral concern that is larger but as intense as Ma's. His knowledge of people is established at the beginning of the novel, in his shrewd, unflattering understanding of the truck driver who gives him a lift, and it widens subsequently with experience on the road. His disdain for the gas station owner precedes his tough moral lecture to the one-eyed junkyard helper and an equally tough lecture to Al. That is to say, Tom is involved. His moral development follows Casy's, with the significant difference that his is the more difficult to achieve. Casy is a relatively simple character; he can express moral concern easily. Tom's emotional numbness following his time in prison does not permit meditation or cancel personality, so the awakening of his moral consciousness on the road is a more rigorous, more painful experience than Casy's time in the desert. Consequently, because of its special quality, Tom's growing awareness of good and evil is a highly credible mirror of the general experience that drives the family toward the group. The logic is paradoxical, but the artistic insight is realized deeply in Tom's circumstantial journey from moral quietism to moral concern for the group.

Enduring all the harsh experiences of their journey, the family gains moral stature and finds that it can function as a unit in the new environment of the road. Its survival in California is a result in part of its redefinition gained on the road.

The interchapters underscore and generalize these particulars. Chapter 14 states the growth of the group concept as a shift in the thinking of the migrants from *I* to *we*. The narrative context is Grandpa's death and the unity of the Joads and Wilsons. Chapter 15 suggests that the Joads' ordeal is a moral experience that affects society at large. Chapter 17 continues the theme that the road furthers the growth of the group concept:

> Every night relationships that make a world, established; every morning the world torn down like a circus. At first the families were timid in the building and tumbling worlds, but gradually the technique of building worlds became their technique. Then leaders emerged, then laws were made, then codes came into being. And as the worlds moved westward they were more complete and better furnished, for their builders were more experienced in building them.

The formation of a group is a "technique" with its basis in the older agrarian order. As with the Joads, the experience of building produces a new moral stature and a redefinition of the family.

In the relation of these events and changes, the narrative chapters and interchapters cohere in an organic unity. Their common theme is movement from and through death to a new life inherent in the group concept. The symbolic level extends the narrative level of movement on the road through time and space. The texture is fully realized. No generalization violates narrative particulars or exists apart from them. Steinbeck's work is careful, convincing, flawless.

The third part—the family's arrival and experience in California—marks an artistic decline. The materials alter and at times the structure is defective.

The chief difference in the materials is an absolute focus on man-made misery. In Oklahoma and on the road, survival can seem to be mainly a struggle against natural conditions. Drouth is the cause of the migration. "The Bank" dispossesses the Okies, but it is not the effective cause of the drouth. In California the struggle is almost entirely against men, and there is no possibility of an escape by further migration. The chief difference in structure stems from Steinbeck's need to begin to think of how to conclude the novel, which presents structural choices and manipulations not present in the first two parts of the novel. For a time the narrative thrust remains coherent, an organic unity disguising these changes.

Grandma's undignified burial establishes the pattern of the family's experience in California. Her pauper's funeral by the state contrasts with the full dignity and free will the family expressed in burying Grandpa. Landless poverty is a moral insult to family pride, and it affects their will to survive. For the moment, as their moral spokesman, Ma expresses a will to recover as quickly as possible for the sake of the future:

> "We got to git," she said. "We got to find a place to stay.
> We got to get to work an' settle down. No use a-lettin' the little
> fellas go hungry. That wasn't never Granma's way. She always
> et a good meal at a funeral."

The conserving lesson of the past is negated by the present economic reality. Ma's brave gesture fails as the family learns that California is a false goal. The imagery associated with California indicates these negations. Peter Lisca and Joseph Fontenrose have pointed to the major biblical parallels in *The Grapes of Wrath,* including those associating California and the Promised Land. The parallels are intensive, even more so than Lisca and Fontenrose suggest, and their function is ironic rather than associative. To begin with, California evokes images of plenty to eat and drink. The ironic fact is that California is the literal reverse of Canaan; there is little to eat and drink, at least for Okies; but California *is* the Promised Land so far as the family's experience there forces the full emergence of the group concept. Appropriately, the family enters California with a foreboding that runs counter to their expectations:

> Pa called, "We're here—we're in California!" They looked dully
> at the broken rock glaring under the sun, and across the river
> the terrible ramparts of Arizona.

They have crossed over, but the physical imagery foreshadows their actual human environment. The land is green across the river, but the biblical lists of landscape features are framed by the fact that they have been carrying Grandma's corpse. The human reality of California life is a living death, as the first camp, the Hooverville, suggests: "About the camp there hung a slovenly despair," everything is "grey" and "dirty," there is no work, no food, and no evident means of overcoming "despair." The deadly economic reality is explained by a young man in the Hooverville, when Tom asks why the police "shove along" the migrants:

> "Some say they don' want us to vote; keep us movin' so we
> can't vote. An' some says so we can't get on relief. An' some
> says if we set in one place we'd get organized."

That reply announces the political solution, the humanly possible way of countervailing power through organization. But the words are programmatic, not a revelation of character.

The difference in materials and in structure begins to appear at this point. The root of the matter is that Steinbeck is so compelled by the documentary facts that he permits their narration to take precedence over the central theme of the family's transformation into the group. And in moving the novel toward an affirmation of life in response to the facts, Steinbeck allows the Joads' experience in California to become a series of allegorical details within a panoramic structure. The narrowed scope of the materials and the schematic handling of the structure are visible in nearly every event in this part of the novel.

Casy's alternative to "despair," sacrificing himself for "the people," is almost wholly an allegorical solution. It is so abstractly schematic that at first none of the family understands its meaningful allegorical force— that loss of self leads to the group concept and thus to power to enforce the will of the group. Instead, the narrative is largely an account of the family's efforts to avoid starvation. The phrase "We got to eat" echoes through these concluding chapters. Ma's changing attitude toward hungry unknown children is ambiguous: "I dunno what to do. I can't rob the fambly. I got to feed the fambly." Ma grows more positive, later, when she is nagged by a storekeeper in the struck orchard:

> "Any reason you got to make fun? That help you any?" . . .
> "A fella got to eat," he began; and then, belligerantly, "A fella got a right to eat." "What fella?" Ma asked.

Ma asserts finally that only "the poor" constitute a group that practices charity:

> "I'm learnin' one thing good," she said. "Learnin' it all a time, ever' day. If you're in trouble or hurt or need—go to poor people. They're the only ones that'll help—the only ones."

"The poor" are identified with "the people," who, in turn are the emerging group. Their purity is allegorical, and, in its limitation, incredible. Steinbeck's handling of "the poor" in *In Dubious Battle* is much less schematic, and therefore far more credible. In general, romanticizing "the poor" is more successful in an outright fantasy like *Tortilla Flat* but Steinbeck commits himself to a measure of realism in *The Grapes of Wrath* that does not sort well with the allegorical division of "good" from "evil."

Romanticizing "the poor" extends beyond Ma's insight to an idealization of the "folk law" that Tom envisions as the fruit of his own experience in California—at a great distance from the "building" experience on the road:

> "I been thinkin' how it was in that gov'ment camp, how our folks took care a theirselves, an' if they was a fight they fixed it theirself; an' they wasn't no cops wagglin' their guns, but they was better order than them cops ever give. I been a-wonderin' why we can't do that all over. Throw out the cops that ain't our people. All work together for our own thing—all farm our own lan'."

Presenting the reverse of Tom's beatific vision in an interchapter, Steinbeck draws on the imagery of the novel's title:

> This vineyard will belong to the bank. Only the great owners can survive. . . . Men who can graft the trees and make the seed fertile and big can find no way to let the hungry people eat their produce. . . . In the souls of the people the grapes of wrath are filling and growing heavy, growing heavy for the vintage.

It is not vitally important that Steinbeck's prediction of some kind of agrarian revolt has turned out to be wrong. The important artistic fact is that "good," divided sharply, abstractly, from "evil," argues that Steinbeck is not interested in rendering the materials in any great depth. Consider the contrast between the people in the government camp and in the struck orchard. Point by point, the camp people are described as clean, friendly, joyful, and organized, while in the struck orchard they are dirty, suspicious, anxious, and disorganized by the police. Credibility gives way to neat opposites, which are less than convincing because Steinbeck's government camp is presented openly as a benevolent tyranny that averages out the will of "the people" to live in dignity and excludes people unable or unwilling to accept that average.

Neat opposites can gather fictive conviction if they are realized through individuals and in specific detail. There is something of that conviction in specific action against specific men, as when the camp leaders exclude troublemakers hired by business interests to break up the camp organization. There is more awkwardness in the exclusion of a small group of religious fanatics obsessed with sin. An important factor is that these people are genuinely Okies, not tools of the interests; another is that the exclusion is necessary, not realistic, if the secular values of the group concept are to prevail. Allowing for his selection and schematic treatment of these materials, Steinbeck does engineer his manipulated point with artistic skill. Fanaticism is considered a bad thing throughout the novel, both as a religious stance and as a social phenomenon. Tom's first meeting with Casy identifies "spirit" with emotional release, not a consciousness of sin, and Casy announces his own discovery, made during his time in the desert, of a social rather than an ethical connection between "spirit" and sexual excitement. Further, fanaticism is identified repeatedly with a coercive denial of life. Rose of Sharon is frightened, in the government camp, by a fanatic woman's argument that dancing is sinful, that it means Rose will lose her baby. The woman's ignorance is placed against the secular knowledge of the camp manager:

> "I think the manager, he took [another girl who danced] away
> to drop her baby. He don' believe in sin. . . . Says the sin is
> bein' hungry. Says the sin is bein' cold."

She compounds ignorance by telling Ma that true religion demands fixed economic classes:

> "[A preacher] says 'They's wicketness in that camp.' He says,
> 'The poor is tryin' to be rich.' He says, 'They's dancin' an'
> huggin' when they should be wailin' an' moanin' in sin.' "

These social and economic denials of life are rooted in ignorance, not in spiritual enlightenment, and they are countered by the materialistic humanism of the camp manager. So fanaticism is stripped of value and associated with business in its denial of life. The case is loaded further by the benevolent tyranny of the group. Fanatics are not punished for their opinions, or even for wrongdoing. They are merely excluded, or they exclude themselves.

A similar process is apparent in the group's control of social behavior, as when Ruthie behaves as a rugged individual in the course of a children's game:

> The children laid their mallets on the ground and trooped silently off the court. . . . Defiantly she hit the ball again. . . . She pretended to have a good time. And the children stood and watched. . . . For a moment she stared at them, and then she flung down the mallet and ran crying for home. The children walked back on the court. Pig-tails said to Winfield, "You can git in the nex' game." The watching lady warned them, "When she comes back an' wants to be decent, you let her. You was mean yourself, Amy."

The punishment is directive. The children are being trained to accept the group and to become willing parts of the group. The process is an expression of "folk law" on a primary level. There is no doubt that Ruthie learned her correct place in the social body by invoking a suitably social punishment.

Perhaps the ugliness implicit in the tyranny of the group has become more visible lately. Certainly recent students of the phenomenon of modern conformity could supply Steinbeck with very little essential insight. The real trouble is precisely there. The tyranny of the group is visible in all of Steinbeck's instances (its ambiguity is most evident in Ruthie's case), which argues for Steinbeck's artistic honesty in rendering the materials. But he fails to see deeply enough, to see ugliness and ambiguity, because he has predetermined the absolute "good" of group behavior—an abstraction that precludes subtle technique and profound insight, on the order of Doc Burton's reservations concerning group-man. The result is a felt manipulation of values and a thinning of credibility.

Given this tendency, Steinbeck does not surprise us by dealing abstractly with the problem of leadership in the government camp. Since there is minimal narrative time in which to establish the moral purity of Jim Rawley, the camp manager, or of Ezra Huston, the chairman of the Central Committee, Steinbeck presents both men as allegorical figures. Particularly Jim Rawley. His introduction suggests his allegorical role. He is named only once, and thereafter he is called simply "the camp manager." His name is absorbed in his role as God. He is dressed "all in white," but he is not a remote God. "The frayed seams on his white coat" suggest his human availability, and his "warm" voice matches his social qualities. Nevertheless, there is no doubt that he is God visiting his charges:

> He put the cup on the box with the others, waved his hand, and walked down the line of tents. And Ma heard him speaking to the people as he went.

His identification with God is bulwarked when the fanatic woman calls him the devil:

> "She says you was the devil," [says Rose of Sharon]. "I know she does. That's because I won't let her make people miserable. . . . Don't you worry. She doesn't know."

What "she doesn't know" is everything the camp manager does know; and if he is not the devil, he must be God. But his very human, secular divinity—he can wish for an easier lot, and he is always tired from overwork—suggests the self-sacrifice that is Casy's function. The two men are outwardly similar. Both are clean and "lean as a picket," and the camp manager has "merry eyes" like Casy's when Tom meets Casy again. These resemblances would be trivial, except for a phrase that pulls them together and lends them considerable weight. Ezra Huston has no character to speak of, beyond his narrative function, except that when he has finished asking the men who try to begin a riot in the camp why they betrayed "their own people," he adds: "They don't know what they're doin'." This phrase foreshadows Casy's words to his murderer just before he is killed in an effort to break the strike: "You don't know what you're a-doin'." Just as these words associate Casy with Christ, so they associate the leaders in the government camp with Casy. Steinbeck's foreshortening indicates that, because Casy is established firmly as a "good" character, the leaders in the government camp must resemble Casy in that "good" identity.

The overall process is allegorical, permitting Steinbeck to assert that the camp manager and Ezra Huston are good men by definition and precluding the notion that leadership may be a corrupting role, as in *In Dubious Battle*. It follows that violence in the name of the group is "good," whereas it is "evil" in the name of business interests. The contrast is too neat, too sharp, to permit much final credibility in narrative or in characterization.

A still more extreme instance of Steinbeck's use of allegory is the process by which Tom Joad assumes the role of a leader. Tom's pastoral

concept of the group is fully developed, and as the novel ends, Tom identifies himself through mystic insight with the group. Appropriately, Tom
explains his insight to Ma because Tom's function is to act while Ma's
function is to endure—in the name of the group. More closely, Ma's earlier
phrase, "We're the people—we go on," is echoed directly in Tom's assur-
ance when Ma fears for his life:

> "Well, maybe like Casy says, a fella ain't got a soul of his
> own, but on'y a piece of a big one—an' then——" "Then what,
> Tom?" "Then it don't matter. Then I'll be all aroun' in the dark.
> I'll be ever'where—wherever you look. . . . See? God, I'm
> talkin' like Casy. Comes of thinkin' about him so much. Seems
> like I can see him sometimes."

This anthropomorphic insight, borrowed from *To a God Unknown* and
remotely from Emerson, is a serious idea, put seriously within the allegorical framework of the novel's close. Two structural difficulties result.
First, Tom has learned more than Casy could have taught him—that identification *with* the group, rather than self-sacrifice *for* the group, is the truly
effective way to kill the dehumanized "Bank." Here, it seems, the Christ/
Casy, Saint Paul/Tom identifications were too interesting in themselves,
for they limit Steinbeck's development of Tom's insight to a mechanical
parallel, such as the suggestion that Tom's visions of Casy equate with
Saint Paul's visions of Christ. Second, the connection between the good
material life and Tom's mystical insight is missing. There is Steinbeck's
close attention to Tom's political education and to his revival of belief in
a moral world. But, in the specific instance, the only bridge is Tom's sudden
feeling that mystical insight connects somehow with the good material life.
More precisely, the bridge is Steinbeck's own assertion, since Tom's mystical vision of pastoral bliss enters the narrative only as an abstract an-
nouncement on Steinbeck's part.

Characterization is, as might be assumed, affected by this abstracting
tendency. Earlier, major characters such as Tom and Ma are "given"
through actions in which they are involved, not through detached, abstract
essays; increasingly, at the close, the method of presentation is the detached
essay or the extended, abstract speech. Steinbeck's earlier, more realized
presentation of Tom as a natural man measures the difference. Even a late
event, Tom's instinctive killing of Casy's murderer, connects organically
with Tom's previous "social" crimes—the murder in self-defense, for
which Tom has finished serving a prison term when the novel begins, and
the parole that Tom jumps to go with the family to California. In all of

these crimes, Tom's lack of guilt or shame links with the idea that "the people" have a "natural" right to unused land—not to add life, liberty, and the pursuit of happiness—and that "the Bank" has nothing but an abstract, merely legal right to such land. Tom's mystical vision is something else; it is a narrative shock, not due to Tom's "natural" responses, but to the oversimplified type of the "good" man that Tom is made to represent in order to close the novel on a high and optimistic note. Tom is a rather complex man earlier on, and the thinning out of his character, in its absolute identification with the "good," is an inevitable result of allegorizing.

Style suffers also from these pressures. Tom's speech has been condemned, as Emerson's writing never is, for mawkishness, for maudlin lushness, for the soft, rotten blur of intellectual evasion. Style is a concomitant of structure; its decline is an effect, not a cause. Tom's thinking is embarrassing, not as thought, but as the stylistic measure of a process of manipulation that is necessary to close the novel on Steinbeck's terms.

The final scene, in which Rose of Sharon breastfeeds a sick man, has been regarded universally as the nadir of bad Steinbeck, yet the scene is no more or no less allegorical than earlier scenes in this final part. Purely in a formal sense, it parallels Tom's mystical union or identification with the group: it affirms that "life" has become more important than "family" in a specific action, and, as such, it denotes the emergence of the group concept. In that light, the scene is a technical accomplishment. Yet it is a disaster from the outset, not simply because it is sentimental; its execution, through the leading assumption, is incredible. Rose of Sharon is supposed to become Ma's alter ego by taking on her burden of moral insight, which, in turn, is similar to the insight that Tom reaches. There is no preparation for Rose of Sharon's transformation and no literary justification except a merely formal symmetry that makes it desirable, in spite of credibility, to devise a repetition. Tom, like Ma, undergoes a long process of education; Rose of Sharon is characterized in detail throughout the novel as a protected, rather thoughtless, whining girl. Possibly her miscarriage produces an unmentioned, certainly mystical change in character. More likely the reader will notice the hand of the author, forcing Rose of Sharon into an unprepared and purely formalistic role.

Once given this degree of manipulation, direct sentimentality is no surprise. Worse, the imagistic shift from anger to sweetness, from the grapes of wrath to the milk of human kindness, allows the metaphor to be uplifted, but at the cost of its structural integrity. The novel is made to close with a forced image of optimism and brotherhood, with an audacious upbeat that cries out in the wilderness. I have no wish to deny the value or the real power of good men, optimism, or brotherhood. The point is that Steinbeck imposes an unsupported conclusion upon materials which themselves are thinned out and manipulated. The increasingly grotesque episodes (and their leading metaphors) prove that even thin and manipulated materials resist the conclusion that is drawn from them, for art visits that revenge on its mistaken practitioners.

To argue that no better conclusion was available at the time, granting the country's social and political immaturity and its economic innocence, simply switches the issue from art to politics. No artist is obliged to provide solutions to the problems of the socio-politico-economic order, however "engaged" his work may be. Flaubert did not present a socioeducational program to help other young women to avoid Emma Bovary's fate. The business of the artist is to present a situation. If he manipulates the materials or forces them to conclusions that violate credibility—especially if he has a visible design upon us—his work will thin, the full range of human possibility will not be available to him, and to that extent he will have failed as an artist.

We must not exclude the likelihood, not that Steinbeck had no other conclusion at hand, but that his predisposition was to see a resolution in the various allegorical and panoramic arrangements that close out *The Grapes of Wrath;* Steinbeck's earlier work argues for that likelihood.

Yet that is not all there is to John Steinbeck. If he becomes the willing victim of abstract, horrendously schematic manipulations as *The Grapes of Wrath* nears its close still he is capable of better things. He demonstrates these potentialities particularly in minor scenes dealing with minor characters, so the negative force of the imposed conclusion is lessened.

Consider the scene in which Ruthie and Winfield make their way (along with the family) from the flooded boxcar to the barn where Rose of Sharon will feed the sick man. The intention of the scene is programmatic: the children's identification with the group concept. The overt content is the essentially undamaged survival of their sense of fun and of beauty. Significantly, the action makes no directly allegorical claim on the reader, unlike the rest of the concluding scenes.

Ruthie finds a flower along the road, "a scraggly geranium gone wild, and there was one rain-beaten blossom on it." The common flower, visualized, does not insist on the identity of the beaten but surviving beauty in pure nature with the uprooted, starved children of all the migrants. The scene is developed implicitly, in dramatic, imagistic terms. Ruthie and Winfield struggle to possess the petals for playthings, and Ma forces Ruthie to be kind:

> Winfield held his nose near to her. She wet a petal with her
> tongue and jabbed it cruelly on his nose. "You little son-of-a-
> bitch," she said softly. Winfield felt for the petal with his fingers,
> and pressed it down on his nose. They walked quickly after the
> others. Ruthie felt how the fun was gone. "Here," she said.
> "Here's some more. Stick some on your forehead."

The scene recapitulates the earlier scene on the playground of the government camp. Here, as there, Winfield is the innocent, and Ruthie's cruelty
is changed by external pressure (the other children, Ma's threat) to an official
kindness that transcends itself to become a genuine kindness when "the fun
was gone." The observed basis of the present scene is the strained relationship that usually exists between an older sister and a younger brother.
There is no visible effort to make the scene "fit" a predetermined allegorical
scheme. Ruthie's kind gesture leads into Rose of Sharon's, as child to adult,
and both scenes project the affirmative values—the survival of optimism,
brotherhood, kindliness, goodness—that are the substance of the group
concept at the conclusion. The children's quarrel and reconciliation is a
relatively unloaded action, an event in itself. Tom's affirmation is nondra-
matic, a long, deeply mystical speech to Ma. Rose of Sharon's affirmation
is out of character and frankly incredible. Uncle John's symbolic action
derives from his own guilt but expresses a universal anger.

As the scene between the children is exceptional, Steinbeck's development of the flood scene is typical. Allegorical intentions override narrative
power: the family's struggle against the flood is intended to equate with its
surviving will to struggle against hopelessness; Pa, Uncle John, and Al are
exhausted but not beaten. Tom's insight precedes the flood; Rose of Sharon's
agreement to breastfeed the sick man follows it. In the larger frame, neither
extreme of drouth or flood can exhaust the will and the vitality of the
people. The dense texture of these panoramic materials is impressive. They
lie side by side, at different levels of the "willing suspension of disbelief,"
depending on whether they are convincing narrative actions or palpable
links in an arranged allegory. Hence, there is no great sense of a concluding
"knot," an organic fusion of parts; there is no more than a formulated
ending, a pseudoclose that does not convince because its design is an a priori
assertion of structure, not the supportive and necessary skeleton of a realized
context. Here structure and materials fail to achieve a harmonious relationship.

These final scenes are not hackwork. We cannot apply to Steinbeck,
even here, the slurring remark that F. Scott Fitzgerald aimed at Thomas

Wolfe: "The stuff about the GREAT VITAL HEART OF AMERICA is just simply corny." Steinbeck's carefully interwoven strands of character, metaphor, and narrative argue a conscious, skillful intention, not a sudden lapse of material or of novelistic ability. Even in failure, Steinbeck is a formidable technician. His corn, here, if it exists, is not a signal of failed ability.

Steinbeck's feeling that *The Grapes of Wrath* must close on an intense level of sweetness, of optimism and affirmation, is not seriously in doubt. His ability to use the techniques of structure to this end is evident. The earlier novels demonstrate his able willingness to skillfully apply an external structure, to mold, or at least to mystify, somewhat recalcitrant materials. The letter withdrawing *L'Affaire Lettuceburg* suggests that Steinbeck is aware of having that willing skill—"just twisting this people out of shape"—and of having to resist its lures in this most serious work. So for the critic there is a certain horrid fascination in Steinbeck's consistent, enormously talented demonstration of aesthetic failure in the last quarter of *The Grapes of Wrath*.

The failure is not a matter of "sprawling asides and extravagances," or the more extreme motivational simplicities of naturalism, or a lapse in the remarkably sustained folk idiom and the representative epic scope. The failure lies in the means Steinbeck utilizes to achieve the end.

The first three quarters of the novel are masterful. Characters are presented through action; symbolism intensifies character and action; the central theme of transformation from self to group develops persuasively in a solid, realized documentary context. The final quarter of the novel presents a difference in every respect. Characters are fitted or forced into allegorical roles, heightened beyond the limits of credibility, to the point that they thin out or become frankly unbelievable. Scenes are developed almost solely as links in an allegorical pattern. Texture is reduced to documentation, and allegorical signs replace symbolism. The result is a hollowed rhetoric, a manipulated affirmation, a soft twist of insistent sentiment. These qualities deny the conceptual theme by simplifying it, by reducing the facts of human and social complexity to simple opposites.

The reduction is not inherent in the materials, which are rendered magnificently in earlier parts of the novel. The reduction is the consequence of a structural choice—to apply allegory to character, metaphor, and theme. In short, *The Grapes of Wrath* could conceivably have a sweetly positive conclusion without an absolute, unrestrained dependence on allegory. Yet the least subtle variety of that highly visible structural technique, with its objectionably simplified, manipulative ordering of materials, is precisely the element that prevails in the final part of *The Grapes of Wrath*.

Why? Steinbeck is aware of various technical options, and he is able to make use of them earlier in the novel. As we have seen in the previous novels, with the exception of *In Dubious Battle,* Steinbeck draws on allegory to stiffen or to heighten fictions that are too loose—too panoramic—to achieve the semblance of a dramatic structure purely by means of technique. Apparently Steinbeck was not offended aesthetically by the overwhelming artificiality that results from an extreme dependence on allegory. That the contemporary naturalistic or symbolic novel requires a less simple or rigid structure clearly escapes Steinbeck's attention.

On the contrary, Steinbeck is greatly attracted to some extreme kind of external control in much of the immediately preceding work and in much of the succeeding work. During the rest of his career, Steinbeck does not attempt seriously, on the massive scale of *The Grapes of Wrath,* to achieve a harmonious relationship between structure and materials. He prefers some version of the control that flaws the last quarter of *The Grapes of Wrath.*

This judgment offers a certain reasonableness in the otherwise wild shift from *The Grapes of Wrath* to the play-novelettes.

The Grapes of Wrath
and Old Testament Skepticism

James D. Brasch

John Steinbeck's Salinas Valley has always rested in the shade of the mountains of the Old Testament, and the legends of the people of Israel have
frequently charted and illuminated the vicissitudes of his characters. Humble
gestures and heroic achievements in Steinbeck's novels recount the history
of "God's chosen people" as they struggled from the Garden of Eden to
the Promised Land. Frequently, the speech rhythms of Steinbeck's chosen
people echo the stately rhythms of the King James Version of the Old
Testament. Even when he used quotations from the Vedas (*To a God
Unknown*) or *Paradise Lost* (*In Dubious Battle*) as epigraphs for his novels,
the tone, diction, syntax, and characterization were reminiscent of the language patterns of the Old Testament writers. This debt to the old chronicles
of grief and pain has never been more obvious and influential than in *The
Grapes of Wrath* (1939).

The religious, political, philosophical and economic context of *The
Grapes of Wrath* has concerned readers and critics of Steinbeck's work ever
since the novel was published. Jim Casy has usually been accepted as the
articulator of Steinbeck's concern. Recalling the religious mentors in great
nineteenth-century novels by Melville and Dostoevsky, for example, critics
have described the presence of Casy as the fulcrum around which the characters and events revolve. Generally speaking, this has involved the somewhat contradictory assumptions that Casy is a Christ figure and the Joads
(read Judah) represent the Children of Israel returning from exile in Egypt.
On occasion the paradox has been resolved by suggesting that in the face

---

From *San Jose Studies* 3, no. 2 (May 1977). © 1977 by James D. Brasch.

of economic calamity, philosophical issues generally remain unresolved. Rather sentimentally, much of the philosophical speculation has assumed that the lack of resolution could be explained by noting the conflicting echoes of American transcendentalism. Steinbeck, however, was not such a casual writer, and the easy assumption that Casy represents the voice of salvation, even though his initials are "J. C.," fails to recognize and acknowledge the precise nature of Steinbeck's inspiration and focus as he expanded his journalistic reports on the Okies into one of the most powerful social novels ever written.

I am convinced that a careful reading of the text of *The Grapes of Wrath* demonstrates that John Steinbeck was not the great celebrant of American values and assumptions articulated by Emerson and Whitman. When Casy emerged from forty days in the wilderness, it was not for the purpose of reaffirming the oversoul which presumably guided the actions and thoughts of nineteenth-century Americans. Nor was Casy the end of a long line of prophets predicting the ultimate triumph of the afflicted on the basis of salvation and hope articulated by Jesus Christ. Casy returned to question the authenticity and, indeed, the very existence of the God who had apparently abandoned his chosen people. In short, his voice was not one of affirmation and consolation; he was a skeptic. He was not Joshua leading the chosen people to victory or Job affirming his God after "the dark night of the soul" or Jeremiah preaching truth to the dispossessed in exile. And he most certainly was not Jesus Christ. Casy was the despairing man of God who found a little comfort in the pleasures and actions and humour of men. He was not *a* preacher; he was *the* preacher. Casy exemplifies the writer of Ecclesiastes who in Melville's tribute was "the truest of all men," because he wrote "the truest of all books": Ecclesiastes, "the fine hammered steel of woe." (Although a longstanding tradition including this reference in Melville ascribes Ecclesiastes to Solomon (about 1000 B.C.), a more accurate dating places the composition considerably later, probably about 200 B.C. The author remains unknown. He is generally referred to as *Koheleth* (or *Qoheleth*) which is the Hebrew rendering of the Greek *ekklesiastikos* (the leader of an open assembly, or an assembly which embraces what is under the sun). . . . The popular rendering of *Koheleth* is "preacher," the word usually used by the Okies when referring to Casy. For the sake of convenience, I will follow the modern custom of referring to the writer of Ecclesiastes as Koheleth.)

Casy has traditionally and rightly been considered the philosophical centre of the novel. Recognition of his Ecclesiastical origins, however, places a different complexion on the novel. Casy's origins were presented by Tom Joad. Just before Tom leaves his mother because of his impending arrest, the two of them examine their general plight, and Tom tells her about Casy's influence. He recalls a sermon by Casy:

"Says one time he went out in the wilderness to find his own soul, an' he foun' he didn' have no soul that was his'n. Says he foun' he jus' got a little piece of a great big soul. Says a wilderness ain't no good, 'cause his little piece of soul wasn't no good 'less it was with the rest, an' was whole. Funny how I remember. Didn' think I was even listenin'. But I know now a fella ain't no good alone."

Casy's reference to a "little piece of a great big soul" is generally considered as a folk rendering of Emerson's oversoul, "within which everyman's particular being is contained and made one with all other; that common heart." Tom's passage, however, did not end there. Steinbeck carefully emphasized Casy's relationship to the writer of Ecclesiastes in the passage that followed. Tom went on:

"He spouted out some Scripture once, an' it didn' soun' like no hell-fire Scripture. He tol' it twicet, an' I remember it. Says it's from the Preacher."
"How's it go, Tom?"
"Goes, '*Two are better than one, because they have good reward for their labor. For if they fall, the one will lif' up his fellow, but woe to him that is alone when he falleth, for he hath not another to help him up.*' That's part of her."
"Go on," Ma said. "Go on, Tom."
"Jus' a little bit more. '*Again, if two lie together then they have heart; but how can one be warm alone? And if one prevail against him, two shall withstand him, and a three-fold cord is not quickly broken.*' "
"An' that's Scripture?"
"Casy said it was. Called it the Preacher." . . .
"An' I got to thinkin', Ma—most of the preachin' is about the poor we shall have always with us, an' if you got nothin', why, jus' fol' your hands an' to hell with it, you gonna git ice cream on gol' plates when you're dead. An' then this hear Preacher says two get a better reward for their work." [My italics.]

"The Preacher," of course, is the author of Ecclesiastes. The italicised passages are verses 9–12 of chapter 4, where the Old Testament Preacher reflects on the obstacles to happiness especially as they are related to labour and wealth. Tom realizes that Casy's quotation of the Preacher represented a departure from the opiates provided by complacent Southern preachers whose platitudinous efforts amounted to duplicitous apologia for the exploitive economic system. "Ice cream on gol' plates when you're dead" is no solution for Tom, Casy, or John Steinbeck in the face of the abuse of the workers and their families. Casy, like the Preacher in Ecclesiastes, teaches Tom that there is more consolation in the warmth and comfort of another human being than in all the consolations of religion and transcendental philosophy. Actually, the introduction of Casy in chapter 4 is, broadly speaking, a summary of the events and attitudes described in Ecclesiastes.

Casy's earthy diction was sometimes upsetting to conventional critics who were reluctant to consider Casy's religious and philosophical orientation, but Casy merely reflects his Old Testament origins. Both the Old Testament sage and Casy realized that one of their chief problems was to seek out "acceptable words" (12:10) in order to explain their disillusionment to their followers and still remain their leaders. The old words of Israel's greatness and, evidently, nineteenth-century America were insufficient. The language of Emerson was of little concern to the Okies trapped in the dust bowls of Oklahoma.

Casy's involvement with the Okies has always given rise to some skepticism just as the Old Testament Preacher's indulgences (see Eccles. 2:10, "I withheld not my heart from any joy") led to God's displeasure. Whether he was participating in militant actions or being oversolicitous of one of the attractive women on the journey, Casy had a way of rationalizing his involvement. Casy's human concerns which refuse to be intimidated by theological orthodoxy or "puritanical" tradition are not unlike Koheleth's reminiscences about his earlier life. He writes, for example:

> I commended mirth, because a man hath no better thing under
> the sun, than to eat, and to drink, and to be merry: for that shall
> abide with him of his labour and the days of his life, which God
> giveth him under the sun.

Casy also ponders his sexual interests in the light of his emphasis on proletarian concerns, as did the Old Testament writer (7:20, for example). Casy analyzes himself:

> "I use to think it was jus' me. Finally it give me such a pain
> I quit an' went off by myself an' give her a damn good thinkin'
> about. . . . I says to myself, 'What's gnawin' you? Is it the

screwin'?' An' I says, 'No, it's the sin.' . . . I says, 'Maybe it
ain't a sin. Maybe it's just the way folks is. Maybe we been
whippin' the hell out of ourselves for nothin'.' . . . There ain't
no sin and there ain't no virtue. There's just stuff people do. It's
all part of the same thing. And some of the things folks do is
nice, and some ain't nice, but that's as far as any man got a right
to say."

The diction is unbiblical, but the tone and substance recall the result of
Koheleth's introspection: "For there is not a just man upon earth that doeth
good, and sinneth not" (7:20). As Koheleth considered the distinctions
between good and evil in his own life and in the history of the Israelites,
the only conclusion he recorded was the one which Casy and the migrant
workers ultimately adopt: "God hath made man upright; but they have
sought out many inventions" (7:29).

Steinbeck, however, not only patterned his itinerant preacher on the
Old Testament Preacher but was influenced by the general philosophical
disposition of the Old Testament skeptic in at least three areas. In the first
place, Steinbeck's proletarian emphasis closely parallels the Old Testament
lament for the exploited workers in Israel. Secondly, the titular emphasis
promising that the "grapes of wrath" are ready for the harvest—that oppression leads inevitably to violent conflict—stems from Koheleth's warnings.
Finally, and perhaps most revealing, Steinbeck's attempts to find a solution
to the conflict clearly reflect the admonitions of the Old Testament sage:
the most practical solution to economic and political tyranny is to be found
in compassion and sympathy and human understanding. An examination
of these three aspects of the novel in addition to consideration of the theological origins and pronouncements of the unorthodox preacher, Jim Casy,
reveals Steinbeck as a writer profoundly influenced by the wisdom of Old
Testament skepticism especially as it is recorded in Ecclesiastes.

Proletarian concern as recorded in Ecclesiastes was the result of the
problems of the United Kingdom of Israel which led to its division into
the kingdoms of Judah and Israel in about 1000 to 900 B.C. Earlier historians
(Samuel and the writer of Kings and Chronicles, for example) had extolled
the victories and triumphs of the former heroes of Israel such as Moses,
Joshua, and David which led to great wealth and prosperity for the faithful.
Hard times had come to the children of Israel, however, and Koheleth set
his task to speculate on the true worth of man in the light of Israel's former
glory. Somewhat reluctantly he recognized that he had to provide consolation for the dispossessed, because the Israeli dream, like its American

counterpart, was not always apparent or symbolized in the natural landscape and its rulers. Ecclesiastes was not, therefore, a book of Psalms or a chronicle of the successful kings of Israel. Koheleth philosophized that "in much wisdom is much grief: and he that increaseth knowledge increaseth sorrow" (1:18). Moreover, love and concern for his people and their labours led Koheleth to recognize that his source of power as a leader or convener in the assembly (i.e., a preacher) lay in his own dependency on the labour of the people: "the profit of the earth is for all: the king *himself* is served by the field" (5:9). All riches, therefore, are derived from the labour of the people of Israel.

Accordingly there are many references to the proletarian point of view in Ecclesiastes. Koheleth recorded that "All things are full of labour" (1:8) and that since there is "no new thing under the sun" (1:9) labour becomes the means whereby progress and quality may be evaluated. As a result, Koheleth argues that man should "rejoice in his own works; for that *is* his portion" (3:22). If man is temporarily disheartened because he is dispossessed, he should be gratified in the knowledge that "the profit of the earth is for all" (5:9). Moreover, the quiet humor of the labourer will serve to preserve his sense of dignity and self-respect: "The sleep of a labouring man *is* sweet, whether he eat little or much: but the abundance of the rich [man] will not suffer him to sleep" (5:12). Finally, because man has "no preeminence above a beast" and returns to dust like the beasts, there can be "nothing better, than that a man should rejoice in his works" (3:19–20).

Just as the Old Testament Preacher realized that the common labourers' real remuneration lay in the satisfactions which they received from honest toil, so Steinbeck's characters consoled themselves with thoughts of their ultimate survival and at least partial triumph. Just as Koheleth recognized that "There is no end of all the people" (4:16), Ma cautions Tom in one of the focal passages of the novel:

> "Easy," she said. "You got to have patience. Why, Tom— us people will go on livin' when all them people is gone. Why, Tom, we're the people that live. They ain't gonna wipe us out. Why, we're the people—we go on."

When Tom asks her how she knows this, her faith triumphs over his skepticism as she answers, "I don't know how," and this intuitive assertion leaves the Joads in a mystical relation to their surroundings from which they gain strength even in moments of intense despair. Considered in the light of Ecclesiastes, the passage reflects a proletarian recognition of the importance of labour to the kingdom of Israel and not some vague echo of

tents come out. The two men squat on their hams and the women and children listen. Here is the node, you who hate change and fear revolution. Keep these two squatting men apart; make them hate, fear, suspect each other. Here is the anlage of the thing you fear. This is the zygote. For here "I lost my land" is changed; a cell is split and from its splitting grows the thing you hate— "We lost *our* land." The danger is here, for two men are not as lonely and perplexed as one. And from this first "we" there grows a still more dangerous thing: "I have a little food" plus "I have none." If from this problem the sum is "We have a little food," the thing is on its way, the movement has direction. Only a little multiplication now, and this land, this tractor are ours. The two men squatting in a ditch, the little fire, the side-meat stewing in a single pot, the silent, stone-eyed women; behind, the children listening with their souls to words their minds do not understand. The night draws down. The baby has a cold. Here, take this blanket. It's wool. It was my mother's blanket—take it for the baby. This is the thing to bomb. This is the beginning—from "I" to "we."

Later in the novel, Steinbeck repeated this theme of consolation in human solidarity as he described the attempts of the farmers to console each other after the long day's trek:

In the evening a strange thing happened: the twenty families became one family, the children were the children of all. The loss of home became one loss, and the golden time in the West was one dream. And it might be that a sick child threw despair into the hearts of twenty families, of a hundred people; that a birth there in a tent kept a hundred people quiet and awestruck through the night and filled a hundred people with the birth-joy in the morning. A family which the night before had been lost and fearful might search its goods to find a present for a new baby. In the evening, sitting about the fires, *the twenty were one. They grew to be units of the camps, units of the evenings and the nights.* [My italics.]

It is important to note that in the midst of Steinbeck's most intense criticism of the corruptions of the American system, the strongest note of hope and proletarian solidarity stems not from Marx, Emerson, Whitman or Jesus Christ, but from the Old Testament skeptic. "For to him that is joined to all the living there is hope: for a living dog is better than a dead lion" (9:4).

Jim Casy's exaggerated, perhaps evangelical plea for a unified mankind is, therefore, a positive celebration of mankind's communion in the face of an economically demeaning isolation and exploitation. The Oklahoma preacher tells his fellow sinners that once in the wilderness he was forced to reconsider his religious assumptions. The result is a gentle sermon, perhaps the key to the entire novel. Casy summarizes the Ecclesiastical emphasis on proletarian insights, predicts inevitable economic conflict, and prescribes the compassionate human solutions and understandings which constitute Steinbeck's attitude toward the oppressed Okies. Like Jesus, Casy found himself in the wilderness, but he makes some nice distinctions which critics have formerly ignored:

> *I ain't sayin' I'm like Jesus,* the preacher went on. But I got tired like Him, an' I got mixed up like Him, an' I went into the wilderness like Him, without no campin' stuff. Nighttime I'd lay on my back an' look up at the stars; morning I'd set an' watch the sun come up; midday I'd look out from a hill at the rollin' dry country; evenin' I'd foller the sun down. Sometimes I'd pray like I always done. On'y I couldn' figure what I was prayin' to and for. There was the hills, an' there was me, an' we wasn't separate no more. We was one thing. An' that one thing was holy. . . . I got thinkin' how we was holy when we was one thing, an' mankin' was holy when it was one thing. An' it thinkin' how we was holy when we was one thing, an' on'y got unholy when one mis'able little fella got the bit in his teeth an' run off his own way, kickin' an' draggin' an' fightin'. Fella like that bust the holiness. But when they're *all workin' together,* not one fella for another fella, but one fella kind of harnessed to the whole shebang—that's right, that's holy. [My italics.]

Here is no triumph of American transcendental self-reliance but rather a wise and gentle teacher reminiscing on the sources of strength and consolation for these latter day Israelites. He even goes on to apologize for the abstractness of the word "holy." Its meaning is closer to home. He concludes his prayer: "I can't say no grace like I use' ta say. I'm glad for the holiness of breakfast." This conclusion to the prayer is preceded by a gentle reminder of Koheleth's disdain for the meaningless repetitions which characterize the participation of many people at divine services. Steinbeck notes that the Joads "had been trained like dogs to rise at the 'amen' signal and as a result kept their heads bowed no matter what their preacher/guest suggested. Whatever else the passage suggests, it must qualify many of the heroic attributes which critics have assumed from the Joads' biblical origins. For the dispossessed Okies, there was nothing more holy than a comfortable breakfast. The tangible experience is holy; the abstract consolation is meaningless. Casy's intense humanity is reminiscent of Melville's sympathies which he too portrayed as a "wanderer" from the Old Testament searching for peace. This is the element of Steinbeck's identification with the Old Testament skeptics which has been most consistently ignored by Steinbeck critics in spite of Casy's definitive disclaimer and directive:

> "No, I don't know nobody name' Jesus. I know a bunch of stories, but I only love people. . . . Why do we got to hang it on God or Jesus? Maybe . . . it's all men an' all women we love; maybe that's the Holy Sperit—the human sperit—the whole shebang."

There are, perhaps, some superficial similarities between Emerson, Whitman and the American pragmatists on the one hand and the writer of Ecclesiastes on the other. These similarities—the self-reliant common man, the mass democracy of Whitman and man's natural progress towards success—must be replaced by a more skeptical demeanor when the plight of the Joads is considered in the light of the Old Testament writer. One detects, perhaps, in the parallel to Ecclesiastes an attitude suggestive of Fitzgerald's *Omar Khyyám* or Nietzsche's *Thus Spake Zarathustra,* and certainly Steinbeck's interpretation of the Joads' experience must take its place with the skeptical tradition of Hawthorne, Melville, Mark Twain, Hemingway and Faulkner rather than with the apologists for American transcendentalism. Progress for both the Joads and the children of Israel was virtually impossible within the eternal cycles of nature and human fallibility, catalogued by Koheleth and Steinbeck as they pondered economic and social disaster in an inscrutable universe.

Primarily Steinbeck was interested in questioning the arrogance of the American economic system with its emphasis on the triumph of the individual. His warnings understood in the light of Ecclesiastes urge a suspicious attitude toward any system which produces victims by the thousands. Probably the most important result of this adjusted reading of Casy's mission is to realize that like Koheleth, Steinbeck's intent is philosophic rather than religious. Casy as a Christ figure leads to an interpretation of *The Grapes of Wrath* as a recognition of the ultimate American victory which Steinbeck, by his emphasis on Ecclesiastes, clearly did not intend. Rose of Sharon's final gesture is not, therefore, symbolic of any ultimate triumph or of better times to come. But as a gesture it is important in itself. It has profound meaning when considered in the light of:

> The thing that hath been, it is that which shall be; and that which is done is that which shall be done; and there is no new thing under the sun. . . . There is no remembrance of former things; neither shall there be any remembrance of things that are to come with those that shall come after.
>
> (1:9,11)

Unlike Jesus, Casy knows that there is no new thing under the sun, there is no good news for the morrow and there are only the humours and labours of the people on which to base a structure for survival.

Flat Wine from *The Grapes of Wrath*

Floyd C. Watkins

A character in fiction is known in part by his relationship with things; he is defined by the clutter of his world. If the things are vague or false, the character is unlikely to be genuine. In a novel with sparse details, the people usually share the vagueness of the environment. Nature may be a large part of the raw materials of fiction. When an author does not know the natural objects of the world he is writing about, then he also gets the manufactured products and the people wrong. A skyscraper or a horse trough or a churn helps to make characters what they are. A writer who does not know a world well should not write about it. But that is precisely what Californian John Steinbeck did in *The Grapes of Wrath* when he wrote about Okies, a people he did not know.

The effect on fiction of an author's ignorance is difficult to measure. It may also be difficult for a critic who is ignorant of a culture to try to interpret fiction about it. One who knows a country or small-town culture can perhaps understand the mores of another country people better than he can understand his own city kinsmen. A rural southerner might read a novel about a Pueblo Indian with more comprehension, for example, than he would have of the urban world of *Herzog*. Can a critic who does not know the culture of the people discussed by an author tell whether or not the author knows that culture? What can he measure by? Some critics presume to judge the truth of fiction when they do not know its background. Reviewers of *The Grapes of Wrath*, for example, thought it was "true"—"great art" and "great sociology." Can a critic or a reader who is well acquainted with a folk culture of his own measure a writer's accuracy when the writer treats a culture foreign to the critic? How long must a writer study an alien culture before he can write about it? Can he acquire such knowledge merely from books? These questions, of course, can be only pondered, not answered.

"Genuine history," Hippolyte Taine has written, "is brought into existence only when the historian begins to unravel, across the lapse of time, the living man, toiling, impassioned, entrenched in his customs, with his voice and features, his gestures and his dress, distinct and complete as he from whom we have just parted in the street" (*History of English Literature*). The novelist and the critic after him may have to cross a barrier of place or culture instead of time as the historian does, but the distance may be just about as great. The novelist is as subject to error as the historian. Hawthorne maintains that a romance must be true to the human heart. Likewise, a social novelist must be true to the cultural as well as to the human. Steinbeck has written what poses as a study in fiction of social reality, but the facts are wrong. Can a credible truth of the heart be embodied in cultural untruth? As *The Grapes of Wrath* is often false and vague, so the characters are false also.

People in a small town or the country are never truly pleased to be the subject of fiction. Mountaineers have objected to James Dickey and Thomas Wolfe, Mississippians to William Faulkner, Indians to Scott Momaday. Many Oklahomans have been infuriated by what they regarded as the insult of *The Grapes of Wrath*. They attacked it on social, factual, and moral grounds, but most of them did not point out many of the specific errors. Lyle H. Boren used the *Congressional Record* to object to the facts: Steinbeck "had tractors plowing land of the Cookson Hills country where there are not forty acres practical for tractor cultivation. He had baptisms taking place in the irrigation ditches in country near Sallisaw, Oklahoma, where an irrigation ditch has not run in the history of the world." But the congressman did not consider his people exposed with justification. "The truth is," he said, "this book exposes nothing but the total depravity, vulgarity, and degraded mentality of the author." Grampa longs to go to California, where he can have enough "grapes to squish all over his face" while in Sallisaw, Oklahoma, he already lives "in one of the greatest grape growing regions in the nation." Frank J. Taylor has disputed almost all the social details about the lives of the migrant workers in *The Grapes of Wrath*—their food, shelter, medical treatment, wages. His bias seems as strong as Steinbeck's when he defends California businesses and governments. Carey

McWilliams, on the other hand, writes that "the LaFollette Committee came along in 1939 and verified the general picture of conditions in the state as set forth in *The Grapes of Wrath*."

Most of Steinbeck's errors about Oklahoma and country people like the Joads have never been pointed out. Some of the mistakes are entirely factual; that is, they can be proved wrong without involving any critical judgment. Including the three errors above, *The Grapes of Wrath* contains nearly twenty plain linguistic and factual inaccuracies:

In the dust bowl "ant lions started small avalanches." Native Oklahomans do not know what ant lions are. Like southerners instead of Californians, they call them doodlebugs.

The famous old "land turtle" which crosses the highway early in the novel is also not native to Oklahoma. The Joads would have called him a terrapin.

Steinbeck's "land turtle" has an armored tail, a biological impossibility. Armadillos have armored tails, but not "land turtles."

Steinbeck's vocabulary is sometimes wrong. By a far stretch of the imagination, a coyote might squawk. But flies do not roar.

Tom Joad would not speak of a "leg" of port, a wrong term for the meat. It should be ham or shoulder.

Ma Joad says salting down meat is woman's work, but that task belongs to men on an Oklahoma farm.

Muley eats prairie dogs in eastern Oklahoma, where prairie dogs have never lived.

Tom Joad wears a coat as he walks on the highway in hot weather, and Muley wears "an old black suit coat" over his "blue jeans," which he would call overalls or overhalls. The dress is authentic, but not in this season. Two Oklahomans told me that no one would wear such clothing except a preacher or an idiot.

The driver of a truck looks out at cornfields and sees that "little flints shoved through the dusty soil." First, the perspective is wrong. The driver could not see them from a truck moving on the road. Furthermore, small flints are not visible through plowed and dusty earth. I have hunted arrowheads in plowed fields in Oklahoma. They are not visible until after a rain, and obviously there had been no rain in the dust bowl in *The Grapes of Wrath*.

The truck driver has had a course in mind-training. After he passes someone on the road, he tries to remember "ever'thing about him, . . . how he walked an' maybe how tall an' what weight an' any scars." Scars would not be visible from a passing truck.

When Muley comes toward Tom Joad and Casy, they "can't see 'im for the dust he raises." Oklahomans who remember dust bowl storms say that you could hardly see a man for the dust, but Muley is not in a storm, and a walking man did not raise that much dust.

Wages are wrong. Tractor drivers in the novel were paid $3.00 a day. Actually, $1.50 would have been good pay for the time.

The Joads have chopped cotton for "fifty cents a clean acre," but that is not the custom. People chopped by the day rather than by the acre.

After Uncle John is baptized, he "jumped over a feeny bush as big as a piana." Feeny bushes are not known to Oklahomans, and I have not been able to find out what one is. Raymond John Taylor, an Oklahoman and a biologist, tells me that a typical bush at a creek where a baptizing occurred would be a button bush. A novelist writing authentically about a region would use a bush common to the area but unknown to many other places and then make it visual. Steinbeck does not do that.

Oklahoma has no lobo wolves.

Besides the factual errors, there are a number of improbable occurrences in *The Grapes of Wrath*. An ant runs "into the soft skin inside the shell" of the "land turtle," and the terrapin crushes it. It would be close in there, but not insecticidal. The Joads' house is pushed down by a tractor. I learned of one such occurrence near Caddo, Oklahoma, in the 1940s, but again the event was not sufficiently representative for Steinbeck to use it in fiction aiming at social truth.

The variety of geography and the diversity of cultures in the United States make a single national literature impossible. In a sense there is no national literary history in America, but there are many different ones. Certain things are nationwide; I believe doves appear all over the country. When a novelist uses only objects that are as universal as the dove, he does not describe a region. Steinbeck did not know Oklahoma well enough to attempt to write a novel about it. The particulars he uses are either from California, or universal, or wrong. The Joads are a kind of people that Steinbeck did not know very well; they have individual identities, but they are not peculiarly Oklahoman. Such things as scissortails and horned toads are not found in *The Grapes of Wrath*. Nor are Indians, and it is impossible to travel far in Oklahoma without seeing some of them. The novel here is incomplete if not erroneous. On one occasion Steinbeck publishes his ignorance of his subject. Casy and Tom Joad see a "dry watering trough, and the proper weeds that should grow under a trough were gone." Now Faulkner would know what kind of weeds were there. The botanical life of Yoknapatawpha County is lush with honeysuckle, heaven trees, dog fennel, jimson weeds, wistaria, verbena, and many other particular plants. "Proper weeds" is plain bad writing. In this case Steinbeck did not even provide a dove, much less a scissortail.

→ *The Grapes of Wrath* is sometimes wrong and often vague, but many details also ring true. Much of the nature is right. Water did have "surface dust" after a storm. Jackrabbits do have boils. A hungry man could eat skunk meat after washing the musk off the fur. The anatomy of the hog-killing is right. The gophers and wild oats and the big owl with a "white underside" are native of Oklahoma. Some unusual customs in the novel were practiced by the poor people during the depression. Farmers lashed barbed wire to fence posts with baling wire because they had no money to buy nails or staples. Urine is used as a medicine by Oklahomans. Farmers have urinated on animals to stop bleeding, rubbed urine as a cure on horses' sores, and used urine as a medicine for earache. That "picture of an Indian girl in color, labeled Red Wing," is on a can of Calumet Baking Power, an item once found in every farm kitchen.

→ So what if the facts are wrong and omitted? Does that make the fiction bad? In a way it does because it becomes allegorical, invented. It is fantasy, and it is false. The people are usually wrong in much the same way the facts are. They live in a flat universality instead of among the clutter of their daily lives. Poverty is not an absence of things in the daily world. The poor have different kinds of things from those who are more fortunate, but they may be surrounded with objects which depict them, as in homes in a junkyard. But Steinbeck's Okies are too much without objects.

A comparison of Steinbeck's journeying Joads with Faulkner's journeying Bundrens in *As I Lay Dying* shows the emptiness of the world of *The Grapes of Wrath*. The Bundrens are relatively poor, but they are culturally rich. During Addie's illness and her death and her funeral she is surrounded by children, her husband, neighbors, a doctor, and a minister— all functioning in their personal and ministering roles with the tools and the clothes and the objects that belong to their characters. The long and almost ridiculous cortege moves through the cultural world of Yoknapatawpha County. Grampa and Granma Joad die outside society and their familial cultures. They have been uprooted. They have no funerals, no neighbors, no ritual, no chance to love. This is an essential difference between the life of a yeoman society still functioning in its tradition and the life of an uprooted society thrown out into a world where all the forms are dead and past. In part, the cultural vacuum of the Joads is a thematic representation of the life of migrants. But they had no cultural richness in their life before they left, as the Bundrens did. They live in a void not so much because Oklahomans left their ways at home as because Steinbeck did not know them well in the first place. The Bundrens and Eudora Welty's poor people and Robert Penn Warren's yeoman farmers have more folk manners than a middle-class society. And wandering peoples take their traditions with them. Country people such as the Joads must be given credit in fiction for the gentility they do have. Without all their trappings, they are reduced to caricatures and buffoons. They may also be made ridiculous even when the author is trying to portray them favorably. As Sinclair Lewis, another writer about the ways of the little man, said, "Steinbeck did not quite get those Okies. . . . He got so lousy sentimental he read sounds into their mouths they could never have uttered."

When *The Grapes of Wrath* violates the mores of people like the Joads, the result almost every time is a reduction of the humanity of the characters. Grampa's leaving his underwear unbuttoned and his fly open is a violation of conventions in the rural Protestant ethic, and even if he is "lecherous as always" his misbehavior would not have been tolerated by members of his family, especially the females. Pa's language before his wife and daughter seems incredibly exaggerated when he refers to his lecherous son's "nuts just a-eggin' him on." Grampa calls a brother, a daughter, and a grandson "sons-a-bitches," and that cussword is almost never taken lightly by people of his class and place. Except in foolish and drunken situations, such name-calling usually has dire consequences (as is potentially true in *Light in August* and *As I Lay Dying*). But Grampa's language provokes not even a shrug. For the sake of sensationalism, perhaps, Steinbeck momentarily forgets the abstract philosophical goodness he attributes to most of the migrants, and he does not even allow them the dignity they do possess. Granma has "survived only because she was as mean as her husband." She opposes him "with a shrill ferocious religiosity that was as lecherous and as savage as anything Grampa could offer." After she rips "one of his buttocks nearly off" with a shotgun blast, he admires her. Grampa and Granma "both sleeps in the barn." The humanity of these characters is so utterly destroyed by Steinbeck's treatment of them that no dignity can survive even when they die. They are ruined by a tone of amused tolerance of near-murder with a shotgun. And their manners at the table leave them with no measure of dignity.

> Granma said proudly, "A wicketer, cussin'er man never lived. He's goin' to hell on a poker, praise Gawd! Wants to drive the truck!" she said spitefully. "Well, he ain't goin' ta."

>   Grampa choked, and a mouthful of paste [pork, biscuit, thick
>   gravy] sprayed into his lap, and he coughed weakly.
>   Granma smiled up at Tom. "Messy, ain't he?" she observed
>   brightly.

Actually Steinbeck is demeaning his own characters whom he presumably pities and loves. He is condemning them on social grounds even though
the book thematically protests economic abuse of them. At times Steinbeck's
amused treatment of them is as inhumane or inhuman as the capitalists are
to the migrants. Tom Joad's family are as unloving as they are illiterate
when he spends four years in jail and his mother writes him only a postcard
after two years and then granny sends him a Christmas card a year later.
Yet the Joads should be a writing family. Witness the extensive corre-
spondence between uneducated soldiers and their families during the Civil
War. In other incidents caricature occurs because Steinbeck, unintentionally
perhaps, reveals how his poor people are unfeeling. The truck they travel
in is crowded, no doubt. Yet it is implausible to take all the mattresses and
barrels of pork and cooking utensils yet to be unable to find a place for the
single stationery box of letters and pictures which Ma burns before she
leaves. Surely she could sew the most precious into the mattresses.

That pig that "got in over to the Jacobs' an' et the baby" becomes a
curious social and cultural generalization about poor Oklahomans instead
of being merely a statement of the hardships of their life and the animalism
of pigs. The author may intend no slur on the nature of the human beings
here, but it is conveyed nevertheless. Pigs do not break into houses and eat
babies except in situations too extraordinary for the author to select as
representative details. The reason is that families guard their houses too
well to admit hogs. Basically the episode attacks the humanity of the people
by reflecting on their care of their children. Even if there is a factual prec-
edent, the atrocity is so unrepresentative that it is too sensational for fiction
which intends to be socially true. Here the novel is more like lurid journalism than fiction intending to depict the character of a people.

The same anecdote in two different contexts may produce entirely
different effects. In Old Southwest humor like that written by George
Washington Harris or Johnson Jones Hooper, cruel jokes and brutal fights
are more slapstick comedy than social generalizations. Steinbeck writes tall
tales in *The Grapes of Wrath,* but the overriding social theme cannot be
detached from them. The integrity of the characters is affected and even
destroyed. Steinbeck exaggerates absurdity in supposedly good people as

much as Faulkner does in the evil Snopeses. Worse, he assigns the absurdities to all the people, creating a wide social generalization, and even the good people threaten violence. Albert, for example, visits the city and returns to find that the folks decided that he had "moved away without sayin' nothin'." They stole the stove, beds, window frames, "eight feet of plankin' . . . from the south side of the house." When he returns "Muley Graves was goin' away with the doors an' the well pump." Albert collected his stuff from the neighbors, but not the pillow stolen by Grampa, who said he would "blow his goddamn stinkin' head off if he comes messin' aroun' my pilla."

Steinbeck denies the Joads and their kind the dignity of their religion, and he does it for a social cause. Casy, the approved philosopher and prophet of the novel, believes in a religion of man which permits meaningless sexual promiscuity. Walter Fuller Taylor has argued that "A reader who really 'buys' The Grapes of Wrath has bought . . . an elaborately illustrated and reiterated philosophy of casual sexual indulgence." In the Bible Belt and among southern yeoman whites their education as well as their religious beliefs derive from the close and intimate knowledge many of them had of the Bible. Steinbeck ridicules this knowledge. Tom Joad does not know whether the Bible is the origin of a country saying: "Don't roust your faith bird-high an' you won't do no crawlin' with the worms." Grampa Joad gets the Bible and Dr. Miles' Almanac all "mixed up." Granma has a "ferocious religiosity," yet her ecstatic pentecostal experience, "speaking in tongues," is still going on when she shoots her husband's buttocks nearly off. Religion is thus associated with humorous violence. She ardently desires a blessing at the table, but she has not "listened to or wondered at the words used" for years. Despite a Christ figure or two, every Christian in The Grapes of Wrath is belittled. Steinbeck's animosity to Christianity shows clearly through once when he writes that they "had been trained like dogs to rise at the 'amen' signal." Why dogs instead of monarchs or holy men? How else should they rise and at what other time? There are no alternatives. Steinbeck is objecting to their Christianity rather than the method or time of rising. He attempts to demean it by comparing them to dogs, and yet he has diminished the presumably good people who are his admired and suffering souls.

Steinbeck's derogatory views of fundamental religionists are presented extensively in the novel. The woman religious fanatic at the government camp in California is nearly as evil and destructive as the agents of the large landowners who wish to use the migrants and to destroy those who object.

A preacher virtually makes war on his congregation when he preaches near an irrigation ditch. He "paced like a tiger, whipping the people with his voice, and they groveled and whined on the ground." He shouted, "Take 'em, Christ!" and threw each one in the water. All Steinbeck's Christians are attacked; the only religion he respects is one like his own belief in the "one big soul ever'body's a part of."

Fundamentalists and Christians in fiction do not all deserve contempt. The Reverend Shegog's sermon in *The Sound and the Fury* is probably the best example in fiction of admirable uneducated Christianity, and other such sermons appear in *Mosquitoes* and *Moby-Dick*. James Weldon Johnson, Robert Penn Warren, and Scott Momaday have also created good but plain ministers. Steinbeck uses the rule passed against taking up collections in camp to suggest that all ministers in the camp are interested only in money. Casy's religion of man is more in harmony with Steinbeck's social views. To substitute a kind of biological transcendentalism like that in this novel for religion is not true to the Protestant ways of the characters. Orthodoxy and tradition in Oklahoma are a part of the way of life. There are many irreligious souls, but most of them are skeptics or hell-raising unbelievers or the indifferent. Casy must surely be the only uneducated rural minister converted to Emersonianism who ever lived in Bible-Belt areas like the South and Oklahoma. Tradition, experience, and culture make preachers in these areas fall to the flesh or to the demon rum, not to freethinking. If a preacher did fall as Casy does among a people like the Joads, their own religion would damn him more than one who fell to the flesh.

It seems strange that a novelist of the stature, talent, and humanity of Steinbeck should get the culture, the facts, and the religion as wrong as he did in *The Grapes of Wrath*. The reason may be simple. The tragedies of the dust bowl and the migrant workers grabbed his interest. He set out to write about them with humanity and for a social purpose, but he was too ignorant of his characters' ways. In this book Steinbeck is what Robert Penn Warren has called a "doctrinaire; that is, he appreciated a work of art to the degree in which it supported his especial theory." Mildly, Steinbeck has allowed social purpose to control him as it has some Russian authors and critics, who, naturally enough, admire this novel especially. He was not a great enough artist to be able to put aside his social beliefs and prejudices. The theme and the practice of the novel show that he could not lift himself to that level. *The Grapes of Wrath* resembles those novels which make all good characters white and all bad ones black or vice versa. But Steinbeck does worse than categorize characters by whether they are good migrants or bad capitalists. He did "conspicuous violence to his laborers" because he tried to blend "left-wing . . . dialectics and the country people together." Communal and biological forms of a unified society do not conform to the fiercely Anglo-American culture which has been established in farming areas like eastern Oklahoma.

Steinbeck, the People, and the Party

Sylvia Jenkins Cook

In 1930 Michael Gold, the left wing's literary hit man, provided a vitriolic foretaste of the controversies of the coming decade in his review for the *New Republic* of the works of Thornton Wilder. Gold attacked Wilder for turning his back on the ravages of capitalism in America and for retreating into remote historical settings and decadent religiosity. The *New Republic* was immediately flooded with letters exhibiting such extremities of partisanship on both sides that Edmund Wilson later recognized in the exchange the advent of "the literary class war." In this intellectual milieu—New York in the early 1930s—few young writers could remain unaware of the ardent political debates of the day, the urgent prescriptions for a revolutionary proletarian literature or the immediacy of the social crisis. However, it was at exactly this point in his career that John Steinbeck was farthest removed, geographically, intellectually, and politically from the left-wing ferment in New York. When the literary class war was declared there in 1932, Steinbeck was in California working on *To a God Unknown,* a novel examining the mystical, pagan instincts that inform the relationships of people to the land they tend. Of his two previously published books, one dealt with the adventures of a seventeenth-century Welsh pirate and the other with the propagation of a curse in a utopian western valley. His favorite reading was neither the *New Republic* nor the *New Masses* but Xenophon, Herodotus, Plutarch, and Sir Thomas Malory, and at this time he was beginning to find the greatest stimulus to his intellectual life not in the Marxist dialectic

From *Literature at the Barricades: The American Writer in the 1930s,* edited by Ralph F. Bogardus and Fred Hobson. © 1982 by the University of Alabama Press.

but in the tide pools of the Pacific, where he became something of an expert in marine biology. To borrow some of the terminology with which Michael Gold scourged Wilder, it all seems rather "erudite and esoteric." Yet in 1941, when Michael Gold summarized the literary 1930s at the fourth and final Congress of American Writers, he chose Wilder and Steinbeck to measure the two poles of achievement in that decade, arguing that "what had happened . . . between Wilder and Steinbeck was a revolution of taste, morals, aspirations and social consciousness. American literature and the audience that read it had reached a certain maturity. A people's culture and hundreds of fine novels, plays and poems impregnated with proletarian spirit had battered down the barricades set up by the bourgeois monopolists of literature."

One might well assume that nothing less than a revolution could have caused the author of *Cup of Gold* and *The Pastures of Heaven* to create a novel of such remarkable timeliness and ideological appropriateness for the 1930s as *The Grapes of Wrath*; yet there is no evidence in Steinbeck's fiction, his letters, or the outward course of his life that he underwent any dramatic conversion away from the remote, heroic, and mystical concerns of his early work to the more topical, naturalistic, and political orientation of *The Grapes of Wrath*. What there is ample evidence for is a gradual and logical evolution of the social metaphors in which Steinbeck embodied his biological interests, which caused him to shift his focus from the marine life of the tide pools to the Communist party and thence to the Joad family. This shift was aided not by literary ideologues in New York but by his empirical observations in California, where he spent almost the entire decade. In this environment Steinbeck had the advantage of detachment from the endless wrangling over revolutionary art and posturing over proletarian causes; however, he was also isolated from the significant reaction that was forming, in a writer, for example, like James Agee, against artistic portrayals of squalor and poverty that seemed to pander to a fashionable taste for exposés of suffering. He was more innocent of both ideology and its exploitation than a writer in Agee's world could ever be. Thus the tumultuous reception of *The Grapes of Wrath* bewildered Steinbeck; he had neither anticipated becoming, as he did, an immediate public institution, nor being characterized, as he was, as a liar, a Communist, and a Jew. He had set out to search for fictional vehicles for rather arcane biological theories and had arrived, in the context of a decade of social upheaval, at the heart of the depression's last literary class war.

The artistic stimulus that Steinbeck found in his biological studies is first articulated in a letter to his friend Carlton Sheffield, dated June 21,

1933. The fact that Steinbeck bothered to date a letter with precision indicates that it had an unusual significance for him, and indeed the text is
often incoherently excited. Three years of random scientific observations
had suddenly taken a clear philosophical direction so that he now felt the
urge to seek what he called "the symbolism of fiction" to act as a vehicle
for them. These observations and experiments are derived largely from his
study of the coral insect, but in the context of the United States in the
depression they all have obvious human and political dimensions. There
are three main issues of importance, the first of which he called the group
or phalanx idea. This concerns the properties of a group organism and their
difference from the properties of the individual units that compose the
group. The ideological extension of this interest in the society of the 1930s
is the clash of totalitarianism and individualism, communal and selfish
behavior. The second concern is with the advantages and disadvantages of
nonteleological thinking; in this area Steinbeck's friend and mentor, Ed
Ricketts, urged on him the value of constantly seeking to understand and
accept what is, rather than a "preoccupation with 'changes and cures' "—
that is, the role of the detached scientific questioner rather than the advocate
of a cause. This issue manifests itself not only in the technique of Steinbeck's
fiction, where he experiments with the idea of having what he calls "no
author's moral point of view," of being "merely a recording consciousness," but also in his version of naturalism, wherein the best-laid schemes
of mice and men are inevitably destined to defeat. Steinbeck was not optimistic about dreams of a more perfect future, yet in the 1930s, the alternative pattern of American pragmatism, of limited and nonidealistic
thinking, seemed increasingly inadequate to deal with the magnitude of the
social crisis. The last of Steinbeck's biological themes is a sense of the unity
and interdependency of all life forms and their environment. It appears early
in Steinbeck's fiction as an instinctive veneration of the natural world by
man; however, when this kind of pantheism is placed in the contemporary
context of the decay of agrarian life, the mechanization, industrialization,
and despoilage of land, it clearly may provoke political as well as religious
responses. None of these biological concerns ever became systematized for
Steinbeck into rigid theories; they are constantly reexamined in his fiction
in changing circumstances. However, the fact that these circumstances include Communist efforts to organize a strike among fruit-pickers and the
exploitation of migrants who are forced off their land lures the reader of
Steinbeck to measure him against the orthodoxies of his time, even if his
progress there was oblique and unorthodox.

Steinbeck's interest in the phenomenon of group behavior was certainly not new to American fiction, as Mark Twain's description of the mob in *The Adventures of Huckleberry Finn* will testify: "The pitifulest thing out is a mob . . . they don't fight with courage that's born in them, but with courage that's borrowed from their mass." In the 1930s a more positive characterization of group behavior emerged in the many proletarian novels that dealt with the solidarity of the union, where workers could acquire dignity, strength, and power, all inaccessible to the exploited and impotent individual. What distinguishes Steinbeck's interest in group man from either of these examples is his reluctance to attach any moral judgment to the group phenomenon. In his original letter describing his fascination with the possible manifestations of the group, he writes that "Russia is giving us a nice example of human units who are trying with a curious nostalgia to get away from their individuality and re-establish the group unit the race remembers and wishes. I am not drawing conclusions." By the following year he had begun work on what he called "the Communist idea" which was to become *In Dubious Battle*. That Steinbeck's stated intentions for this novel are not wholly congruent with the effect it achieves is a measure of the gap in Steinbeck between the behavioral theories of the amateur biologist and the broader perspective of the artist, a gap that was to increase through-out the 1930s. He denied that the novel was anything other than a harsh scientific investigation of "man's eternal warfare with himself," saying, "I'm not interested in strike as means of raising men's wages, and I'm not interested in ranting about justice and oppression. . . . I wanted to be merely a recording consciousness, judging nothing, simply putting down the thing." Steinbeck felt that he had found in this study of the manipulations of a group of migrant workers by Communist party organizers an ideal crucible for testing the development of his group-man notions; but as soon as the material took form in a specific historical setting, Steinbeck's more complicated sympathies and prejudices altered the novel's supposed im-partiality: it is not propaganda, but it clearly illustrates the problems of nonpartisanship.

Group man in *In Dubious Battle* is illustrated by a crowd of striking apple-pickers in the Torgas Valley in California. Individually, they are as far as is imaginable from the conventional image of the deserving poor: they are lazy, careless, cruel, cowardly, envious, and selfish. They refuse to cooperate voluntarily to secure even minimal sanitary arrangements for their camp. The men exploit the women sexually, and the women provoke the men to blood lust. It could never be said of these strikers, as it was of the Okies in *The Grapes of Wrath,* that they bear only the physical but not the spiritual stigmas of poverty and injustice. Yet Steinbeck refuses to indulge in such rationalizations here for the repulsive qualities of his pro-tagonists. When these same men are unified into a group animal by the skill of Mac, the Communist organizer, the new creature is powerful, reckless of danger, savagely ferocious. It is neither more nor less decent than the individuals who compose it, but it is vitally different in many of its attributes. There is no alternative view in the novel of American working men en masse. The two characters who conduct the intellectual debate of the novel over Communist tactics are in complete agreement with this vision of group man though they differ in their responses to it. Mac, the doctrinaire field organizer, sees the group animal as something to be fed and goaded in the service of Communist political ideals; his images for the group are inevitably contemptuous animal analogies. Doc Burton, the "dreamer, mystic, metaphysician" who gives free medical attention to the strikers, but is himself "too God damn far left to be a Communist," sees group man as something to be studied and analyzed in the service of knowl-edge; he rejects Mac's animal images but substitutes for them images of germs and cells that are certainly no less dehumanizing. The only denial in the novel of the totalitarian implications of this vision of human nature comes from the hypocritical president of the Fruit Growers' Association, who has most to gain by it. Yet the brutal detachment Steinbeck professed and aimed at in *In Dubious Battle* is not absolute; while the group animal and its analysts Mac and Doc Burton clearly engaged his intellectual inter-ests, it was not apparently a sufficient vehicle for his less impersonal artistic sensibility. Thus the novel contains two characters, a father and son, who remain completely outside the theoretical scheme of the novel but who clearly have Steinbeck's sympathy. These are the Andersons, who operate a small, independent farm and a low-profit lunch wagon; they are genial, self-reliant, and efficient men who have their livelihoods destroyed because they side with the aims of the strikers. Since they are so much closer than the fruit-pickers to a benevolent image of the people, they suggest a possible evolution for Steinbeck away from the mechanical and faceless mob—the product of his emotional detachment—to the more heroic and dignified people with roots in history, culture, and region who will form the group animal in *The Grapes of Wrath*.

This is not a simple transition from scientific detachment to emotional involvement on Steinbeck's part—it is also a recognition that the context in which the group phenomenon is studied alters its significance. Thus one Marxist critic of *In Dubious Battle* called it the most lifelike and satisfying proletarian novel of the 1930s. The label is false if used in the conventional sense of the term since the novel does not seek to promote the cause of

revolution, but it indicates the partisan nature of Steinbeck's chosen setting—any fiction that dealt with labor activities in the depression and
stopped short of opposing it might incur such a label.

Between the publication of *In Dubious Battle* in 1936 and *The Grapes
of Wrath* in 1939, Steinbeck wrote a short story, "The Leader of the People,"
that may serve to emphasize further how the "fictional symbols" in which
he embodies the group theory can alter its ideological effect. The story is
about an old man who, at one time in his life, had found himself a special
kind of cell in a group organism, much as the Communist Mac had in *In
Dubious Battle*. He had been the leader of a group of westward-trekking
pioneers who had survived a grueling journey across the continent. When
they finally reached the Pacific the leader's function had disappeared and to
his family he has now become a boring and garrulous figure, endlessly
recalling his adventures. The old man is eventually trapped into admitting
the authentic nature of the experience: it was a group phenomenon rather
than a heroic act. "It wasn't Indians that were important, nor adventures,
nor even getting out here. It was a whole bunch of people made into one
big crawling beast. And I was the head. It was westering and westering. . . .
I was the leader, but if I hadn't been there, someone else would have been
the head. The thing had to have a head." However, his grandson Jody, like
the reader of *The Grapes of Wrath,* cannot shake off the heroic associations
of westering. In that novel they are revived forcefully, together with all
the resolution and hope of the earlier pioneers.

Steinbeck presents the movement of the Okies to California as mysterious and biologically determined, but the context of the people and the
evocative associations of their journey recall other, more human standards
by which to judge it. The historical context of pioneering is only one of
the differences in setting between the filthy, cowardly, and brutish workers
of *In Dubious Battle* and the noble and enduring Okies of *The Grapes of
Wrath*—two groups of people who might otherwise seem so contradictory
in their conception as to suggest that Steinbeck radically altered his whole
view of human nature between the two books. The Okies, unlike the
striking fruit-pickers, are presented as victims of a natural disaster as well
as an economic crisis: since the earth has failed them, they must begin anew.
Thus there is an impelling logical reason for their migration that makes it
both sensible and sympathetic. The Okies are also placed in a cultural
tradition that gives dignity and stature to their predicament; they are the
descendants of the people who helped clear and settle the continent, who
fought in the Revolution and the Civil War. They carry suggestions of the

chosen people as they seek for the Promised Land in California. None of these dignifying factors negates the essential biological nature of the mass movement of the group in *The Grapes of Wrath,* but they add an epic and legendary quality to the adventure that suggests that Steinbeck's evolving concern for the migrants has led him to a new and less dispassionate metaphor for his scientific interests.

The group unit itself is given a more varied portrayal in *The Grapes of Wrath*; it is no longer limited to the single feral body of strikers but may be seen in the Joad family moving into unified action to slaughter pigs; it may be a camp of migrants that comes into existence for one night only; it may be a field of cotton-pickers or a chorus of fanatical Jehovites; it may be the massive migratory group, crawling like insects along the highways; or it may be the ultimate macrocosmic group, Manself. These groups, true to their original biological conception, have properties different from those of their individual members: "The bank is something else than men. It happens that every man in a bank hates what the bank does, and yet the bank does it. The bank is something more than men, I tell you. It's the monster." However, with the illustration of such a variety of group formations, Steinbeck also reveals group properties that are clearly differentiated from each other and on which he now appears to make moral and political judgments. The howling, whining, and thumping of the religious enthusiasts does not make an admirable contribution to the life of the people, while the instinctive communal behavior in the roadside camps does; there, "in the evening a strange thing happened: the twenty families became one family, the children were the children of all. The loss of home became one loss, and the golden time in the West was one dream"—this is clearly beneficial to the mutual welfare as laws are established and property shared. The groups continue as in *In Dubious Battle* to respond to emotional goading, but unlike the arbitrary scenes of bloodletting created by the callous and opportunist Communists to stimulate the strikers' lust, in *The Grapes of Wrath* the provocation is completely integral to the situation, and the reader responds to it even before the Okies themselves:

> The people come with nets to fish for potatoes in the river, and the guards hold them back; they come in rattling cars to get the dumped oranges, but the kerosene is sprayed. And they stand still and watch the potatoes float by, listen to the screaming pigs being killed in a ditch and covered with quicklime, watch the mountains of oranges slop down to a putrefying ooze; and in

the eyes of the hungry there is a growing wrath. In the souls of the people the grapes of wrath are filling and growing heavy, growing heavy for the vintage.

Anger changes in this novel from a carefully fostered biological urge to a moral obligation; and the mob man is now labeled Manself, willing to "suffer and die for a concept, for this one quality is the foundation of Manself, and this one quality is man, distinctive in the universe."

Had Steinbeck rested *The Grapes of Wrath* on this ideological refinement of group man, it might well have been a more satisfactory proletarian novel; instead he chose to extend the context of the group not just beyond the biological to the political and moral level, but beyond that to the mystical and transcendental: the final apotheosis of group man in *The Grapes of Wrath* is not to socialist unity but to the oversoul. In *In Dubious Battle*, the subversive Doc Burton had posed the question, "Can't a group of men be God?" only to be rebuffed by the practical Communists; in *The Grapes of Wrath*, when Casy says, "Maybe all men got one big soul ever'body's a part of," there is no spokesman for an opposing point of view. Set in a highly topical situation, *The Grapes of Wrath* shows a keen awareness of man as a political animal, existing somewhere between the tidepool and the stars, but, true to his personal and empirical attitude, Steinbeck refuses to be limited exclusively to that consciousness.

Steinbeck's interest in nonteleology as a way of approaching life and literature was first stimulated by his association with Ed Ricketts at the Pacific Biological Laboratories, and like the group-man theory, it rapidly moves in the fiction far beyond its scientific sources. Ricketts felt that people in a complex universe tended to search for its purpose before they had any comprehension of what it was—they asked the question, Why? before they tried to answer the question, How? Ricketts advocated instead what he called "is" thinking, which sought understanding without judgment and was therefore "capable of great tenderness, of an all-embracingness" that is rare otherwise. Steinbeck's fascination with this theory is indicated by the frequency with which he creates fictional characters who voice Ricketts's opinions: Doc Burton in *In Dubious Battle*; Casy and, to some extent, Ma Joad in *The Grapes of Wrath*; and Doc in *Cannery Row*. But, especially in the novels written in the 1930s, Steinbeck consistently questions the social consequences and dangers of this rather passive view.

Doc Burton is one of the more appealing characters in *In Dubious Battle*; in a world of cruel and self-assured fanatics, he is gentle and tentative in his opinions; in a world of violence and destruction he aids and cures. He serves humanity without judging it; in a partisan setting, he has avoided taking sides. In his many debates with Mac, the Communist, he emphasizes his quest for pure knowledge, uncontaminated either by moral or historical labels: "I don't want to put on the blinders of 'good' and 'bad,' and limit my vision. . . . I want to be able to look at the whole thing." Burton denies beginnings and ends, seeing only constant flux that prevents any practical, goal-oriented action. He is an enigma to Mac, who responds to his arguments with a mixture of revulsion and admiration, "In one way it seems cold-blooded, standing aside and looking down on men like that, and never getting yourself mixed up with them; but another way, Doc, it seems fine as the devil, and clean." Doc's mysterious disappearance from the novel indicates that in this particular dubious battle, when the ranks are drawn, there is simply no place for the man who tries to remain unsullied by partial commitment. To be "fine as the devil, and clean" is also to be intolerably isolated from human endeavor, as his departing remarks in the novel assert: "I'm awfully alone. I'm working all alone, toward nothing."

The Grapes of Wrath traces in more detail the wholesale transformation of two of its heroes, Casy and Tom, and the imminent conversion of the third, Ma Joad, away from "is" thinking to the search for both causes and ends. At the beginning of the novel, the former preacher, Jim Casy, is very much in the nonteleological mold of Doc Burton; he has given up his ministry to study his fellow mortals, of whom he says, nonjudgmentally, "There ain't no sin and there ain't no virtue. There's just stuff people do. . . . And some of the things folks do is nice, and some ain't nice, but that's as far as any man got a right to say." Casy, too, has a sense of living in a directionless flux, but unlike Doc Burton he gradually comes through his experiences to see a meaning and purpose in it—on the road west he observes of the migrants, "They's gonna come somepin outa all these folks goin' wes'—outa all their farms lef' lonely. They's gonna come a thing that's gonna change the whole country." Despite his initial rejection of sin, Casy is soon brought to the assertion that "they's somepin worse'n the devil got hold a the country, an' it ain't gonna let go till it's chopped loose." By the time of his death, Casy appears to have identified what is worse than the devil as California's rampant capitalism, and he gives his life to the ideal of defeating it.

Tom Joad is at first stolidly unimpressed by Casy's vaguely apocalyptic vision of the future; to Casy's admission that he mentally climbs barriers that have not yet been built, Tom replies, "I'm still layin' my dogs down one at a time." However, he is gradually led to realize, much as Steinbeck himself appeared to be doing, the dangers of such aimlessness. When his conversion to social activism comes, it is the result of personal experience rather than the preacher's rhetoric. This is a crucial difference between the radicalism in *In Dubious Battle* and that of *The Grapes of Wrath*: in the earlier novel, a rigid ideology is furthered by the emotional manipulation of the group; in the latter, the people themselves are educated empirically into their new activism. Tom's first advice to Ma Joad when she worries about the future is to "jus' take ever' day," an attitude that is qualified for the reader by the knowledge that it is the product of Tom's prison experiences in a powerless and dependent role. When Ma attempts to live by this ideal, it becomes a struggle to preserve the family unit against its assimilation into any wider group. As the futility of that struggle gradually becomes apparent, Ma, too, finally comes to recognize the need for a new vision of the future. She never relinquishes altogether her concern for the immediate future to the extent that Tom and Casy do, but she knows by the end that if people are ever to exist in more peace and security, it will be because of those who dedicated themselves to a final purpose instead of just "taking every day." Steinbeck's original attraction to the nonteleological view of the scientist is reversed when the fictional symbols in which he embodies it are the peculiar disasters of the depression for people who have formerly dedicated themselves to "is" thinking.

The last of Steinbeck's biological interests that found fictional symbols in his work during the 1930s is his sense of the mystery of ecology and especially of the mutual and sacred dependence of people and land. Like other American writers in the thirties, notably Faulkner and Caldwell, Steinbeck was interested in the special nature of the agricultural bond, since agribusiness and natural disasters seemed about to end it forever. It is explored early in his fiction in the pagan religious context of *To a God Unknown* in 1933; only later in the decade does the topic come to have a political dimension. *To a God Unknown* deals with the mystical union between the farmer, Joseph Wayne, and the homestead he acquires in California. Joseph's cult begins in a simple lust for the land, symbolized in a ritualized mating with it. He glories in its fertility, identifies a tree as the spirit of his dead father, makes sacrificial offerings to the land, and ultimately comes to identify with it so completely that he kills himself in a dry season in the certainty that his blood will water and renew the earth. Although this novel was seen by most critics as a kind of anthropological curiosity, the same identification with the land, both physically and spiritually, is apparent in the more contemporary and realistic Okies in *The Grapes of Wrath*, who affirm that the "place where folks live is them folks."

In *The Grapes of Wrath*, Steinbeck depicts what happens to the land as well as the people when the agrarian bond is broken. The tractors that come on to the land, driven by machinelike men who eat machine-made food, rape the land that had formerly been loved and cause its symbolic death. Thus the banks that drive the people off the land are shown to be committing not only a crime against humanity but also a sacrilege against the religion of agriculture. This attitude is identified by critic Chester Eisinger with Jeffersonian agrarianism, and he argues that, appealing as this philosophy may be, it is certainly an outmoded way of dealing with the problems of the Okies in the 1930s. However, while Steinbeck clearly displays some nostalgia for such notions, he also identifies them as part of the past that is irretrievable; in addition to the banks that tractor the people off the land, there are the dust storms that would ruin their livelihood anyway; their legal or moral right to stay is undermined by nature itself turning against them. The pantheism of the novel is rooted in hunger for fertile, productive land; it is useless to continue to worship land that is already dead, as Muley Graves and Granpa Joad do. Steinbeck demands adaptability as well as resilience in his species of farmers so that even at the nadir of the Joads' suffering in California, when Pa wishes only to return to Oklahoma, Ma insists that California, which has treated them so badly, is nevertheless "better land."

The religious element in Steinbeck's agrarianism that made reviewers of *To a God Unknown* wish that he could find more stable and relevant principles on which to build future novels proves capable in *The Grapes of Wrath* of supporting a highly political and topical thesis: "when property accumulates in too few hands it is taken away. . . . when a majority of the people are hungry and cold they will take by force what they need. . . . repression works only to strengthen and knit the repressed." Land hunger in Steinbeck is from his earliest works both a physical instinct and a religious need; in *The Grapes of Wrath,* when the days of homesteading are past, it becomes also a political principle.

The fact that Steinbeck's biological interests took the direction they did in his fiction in the 1930s is, of course, a direct consequence of the times in which he lived. Although Steinbeck was largely estranged from the cliques of radical literary activists, he was throughout the depression coming into more and more intimate contact with the human suffering it spawned. In 1934 he had written sardonically to a friend in New York, "I am pegged as a pessimistic writer because I do not see the millennium coming." By 1936, after he had done a series of reports for the *Nation* on migrant labor in California, he was writing to the same friend, "There are riots in Salinas and killings in the streets of that dear little town where I was born. I shouldn't wonder if the thing had begun. I don't mean any general revolt but an active beginning aimed toward it, the smouldering." This is a considerable progress in millennialist rhetoric in the space of two years, and what was largely responsible for Steinbeck's rather late awakening was the peculiar experience of California. Since much of the suffering and exploitation there arose as a consequence of the Dust Bowl migration, the exposure and consciousness of it came much later in the decade than the circumstances that gave rise to the main flowering of proletarian literature. By 1938 Steinbeck's letters show a repeated anguished emphasis on the explosive situation in California, the starvation and disease among migrant families, and the sabotaging of all efforts to help them by what he calls the "fascist" utilities and banks. Steinbeck was torn between his desire to write his fury into a work of fiction and a more pressing need to take direct action, "to help knock these murderers on the heads." One of his letters ends, "funny how mean and little books become in the face of such tragedies"; a few days later, he arranged for the proceeds of his articles to buy serum and codliver oil for the migrant children and then concluded in despair, "Of course no individual effort will help." A week or two later, he apparently decided that reporting might be the best medium: "I want to put a tag of shame on the greedy bastards who are responsible for this but I can best do it through newspapers." *The Grapes of Wrath* is thus very firmly grounded in the immediate turmoil of the California scene although it is necessary to add that it was not an immediate product. The first book Steinbeck wrote out of his anger was a bitter satire called *L'Affaire Lettuceburg*; he later rejected it because it was "mean" and "nasty" and, by dealing in half-truths, more likely to cause hatred than understanding. When he began work on *The Grapes of Wrath,* the need to take immediate action had been satisfied by his journalism and personal generosity; the need to vent his rage had been poured into the abandoned propagandistic novel that he knew was bad. Thus into *The Grapes of Wrath* he could distill the more measured results of a whole decade of intellectual and literary apprenticeship with a topic that was almost exclusively apt to his worldly experience.

There is one final factor in Steinbeck's intellectual background that plays an important role in his political novels and indeed, according to his friend Toni Ricketts, was the "real clue to his writing": this was what she characterized as "his hatred of the middle class." This appears to be not so much a class-conscious attitude in a political sense as a preference in cultural and moral values for lower-class people who lived with excess and abjured moderation. The excess might take the form of sexuality, drunkenness, gross appetite, or religious enthusiasm; Steinbeck was not so much interested in the specific manifestation of a zest for life as in abhorring the prudence, prurience, rigidity, and conformity that robbed people of the capacity for heroic conduct or the pursuit of dreams. His earlier, largely unpolitical fiction—*Cup of Gold, The Pastures of Heaven,* and *Tortilla Flat*— had all examined the stultifying effects of respectability, mediocrity, and stability on the human tendency to wildness and eccentricity. Although the Joads in *The Grapes of Wrath* are never so extravagant as the people in these early novels in their appetite and indulgences, they are certainly immoderate and nonconformist. Every member of the family is introduced by a tale of excess, from Tom's murder to Granma's religious ecstasies to Al's tom-catting, Uncle John's binges, and Ma's attack on a peddler with a live chicken. The Joads, however, are also generous, compassionate, and able to restrain their impulses when it is necessary for the common good. They are hardworking, not for acquisition but for survival and the pleasure of performing well. Only in *The Grapes of Wrath* do these qualities become politically class-conscious, since they are deliberately opposed to the "shit-heels"—the worried, insecure businessmen with their languid, discontented wives, rushing across the country to California to indulge in gossip and vicarious living because they no longer have any vitality in themselves. Steinbeck's comments on the decadence of these people, of their pursuit of the artificial and perversion of the natural, come very close to the standard conventions of proletarian fiction, but for him they are very far from being leftist clichés, or a sentimental indulgence in primitivism. They are rather the logical development, in the political atmosphere of the depression, of an early and instinctive prejudice.

When *The Grapes of Wrath* was published, it shocked, offended, and made enemies for Steinbeck, but it also brought him instant fame, offers from Hollywood, membership in the Press Club, and a Pulitzer prize; he was now an acknowledged member of the literary set. He was completely unprepared for such a response. While the novel was in the publication process, he wrote repeatedly warning Viking against a large first edition. His later letters express surprise but little elation at the reception of it; he seems to have been exhausted, both physically and mentally, skeptical of any political action, and wholly disillusioned with the genre in which he had been working: "I've worked the novel . . . as far as I can take it." He loathed the newfound intrusions on his privacy and feared for his future integrity the consequences of "this damnable popularity." He determined to change directions, to abandon fiction altogether for scientific studies, to write a good book that few people would want to read. He foresaw himself becoming what he had so detested—respectable, consistent, satisfactorily assimilated. As with his late and largely empirical conversion to radical politics, Steinbeck needed to feel the actual destructive force of success on himself before he doubted the validity of his particular approach to art. It was a position to which one other notable radical writer had come by the end of 1930s, but for James Agee the revulsion from the public's appetite for aesthetic images of human suffering preceded the writing of his great depression effusion, *Let Us Now Praise Famous Men*. With a topic and a political philosophy remarkably close to Steinbeck's, Agee's work helps to dramatize, by its almost nihilistic originality as well as by its ideological torment, both the advantages and disadvantages of the enduring value of *The Grapes of Wrath*, of Steinbeck's estrangement in California during the 1930s.

Let Us Now Praise Famous Men grew, like *The Grapes of Wrath*, from a specific experience of human suffering and from Agee's background in the depression, which was markedly different from Steinbeck's—at the center of the New York literary and radical world. From that he had acquired a distaste for the chic, left-wing affectation he observed, as well as for the fashionable new relevance of the artist. It was a distaste that led him to reject all the successful literary conventions of the 1930s for a work that he determined would be as unpalatable to the aesthetes of suffering as he could possibly contrive. He succeeded in creating a book that had in its own day no popular appeal and limited critical enthusiasm but has risen steadily in critical estimation ever since, so that it is not unusual now to see it hailed as the greatest literary achievement of the depression. By contrast, the reputation of *The Grapes of Wrath* in America had declined so much that in 1962, when Steinbeck was awarded the Nobel Prize, the *New Republic* rather ungraciously editorialized that it could not in any sense acknowledge that he was a great artist, or even nationally esteemed. Steinbeck's novel had succeeded in the 1930s not merely because of its topicality but also because of the skill with which he had documented the voices and lives of the migrants, the carefully fostered dialectical debate between the chapters and interchapters, the compassion with which the novel demanded a moral response from its readers. In contriving a technique, as well as an ideology, Steinbeck had come to discover the use of conventions such as documentary journalism, folk idiom, multiple protagonists, and ideological irony and symbolism that had become common in the thirties in the fiction of other left-wing writers, but in the eyes of a writer like James Agee, hackneyed and discredited. Steinbeck's isolation from Agee's world permitted his education in the field rather than the radical drawing room; it enabled him to explore his biological interests free of ideological harassment and to evolve new vehicles for them in accordance with his emotional sympathies. Nevertheless, this freedom cost Steinbeck something in the loss of the kind of intellectual stimulus and debate that helped direct Agee towards the creation of a new literature of the left, rather than, as *The Grapes of Wrath* finally seems to be, the climax and culmination of the old. Perhaps, in this sense, Michael Gold's enthusiasm is its most fitting epitaph.

The Enduring Power of the Joads

Donald Pizer

Steinbeck's most famous novel is enshrouded in a number of myths about its origin and nature. Here is a work which appears to be the epitome of the 1930s proletarian novel in that all its good people speak bad English, which sweetens its animal view of human nature with an anomalous mixture of Christian symbolism and scientific philosophy, and which appeals principally on the level of sentimentality and folk humor. *The Grapes of Wrath,* in short, is naturalism suffering the inevitable consequences of its soft thinking and its blatant catering to popular interests.

The Grapes of Wrath is indeed closely linked to the 1930s. Unlike either *Studs Lonigan* or *U.S.A., The Grapes of Wrath* is set entirely within the 1930s and is concerned with a distinctive condition of the depression. The novel is also a work of the 1930s in the sense that it is a product of Steinbeck's artistic maturation during that decade. His first three novels, all of the late 1920s, are marked by excessive fantasy and turgid allegory. In 1930 Steinbeck married Carol Hemmings, met the marine biologist Ed Ricketts, and began to interest himself in economic and social problems. His wife's deep commitment to his career, Ricketts's philosophical naturalism, and the impingement of contemporary social events on his writing seemed to push Steinbeck not into a denial of his earlier "romantic" strain but toward a hybrid form in which symbol making and ideas have a solid base in contemporary life. In the mid-1930s Steinbeck became absorbed in the plight of the migrant farm workers of the central California valleys. He reported their conditions, talked at great length about their ways in the prairie West and California with the sympathetic manager of a government camp, and thus gained an awareness of the substantive detail which crowds *The Grapes of Wrath*.

The Grapes of Wrath is also a depression novel in its often doctrinaire 1930s economic, social, and political ideas. As late as 1960, in a reminiscence of the 1930s, Steinbeck still held a melodramatic view of the decade, one in which Hoover epitomized the forces of social evil and Roosevelt of good. *The Grapes of Wrath* has something of the same character. Evil is epitomized by the great banks and corporations which oppress the common worker and manipulate, by fear, the lower middle class. The California portion of the novel even enacts an American version of European fascism, in which the deputies and vigilantes are proto-fascists and the migrants are hounded Jews. To this 1930s mix, Steinbeck adds an appropriately Marxist interpretation of history and of economic processes. The migrants can be exploited because labor is abundant, the "lesson of history" is that the increasing chasm between the haves and the have-nots will result in revolution, and organization of the masses—from camp sanitation committees to labor unions—is the solution to all social problems.

There is also an element of truth in the view that *The Grapes of Wrath* contains an uneasy amalgam of what Edmund Wilson called "biological realism" and an overapparent Christian symbolism. Few readers today would accept Wilson's remark of 1940 that Steinbeck's characters are "so rudimentary that they are almost on the animal level" or the obsessive concern in the 1950s and early 1960s with biblical parallels in the novel. Nevertheless, the Joads are primitive folk who live close to the natural processes of life, Steinbeck does occasionally indulge in a blatant animism (the turtle crossing the road is a famous example), and the Joads' exodus and Casy's life and death are immediately evocative of Christian myth.

Perhaps the most troublesome matter involving the background of *The Grapes of Wrath* in recent decades has been the relationship between the themes of the novel and the philosophical ideas expressed by Steinbeck in his *Sea of Cortez*. Ostensibly a record of a voyage in 1940 by Steinbeck and Ricketts to study marine life in lower California, *Sea of Cortez* also contains a number of philosophical meditations. The most significant of these is an "Easter Sermon" on the advantages of "non-teleological" or "is" thinking. The non-teleological thinker accepts the fatuousness of man's belief that his will can control events and thus concentrates on understanding experience rather than on judging men. Steinbeck also expresses in *Sea of Cortez* a belief in group identity, an identity which he elsewhere calls the "phalanx."

As individuals, all creatures, including man, are usually weak and un-knowing; as members of a group they can "key in" to the strength and knowledge of the group. A group can thus have a distinctive identity. As Steinbeck wrote in a letter of 1933, when he first became interested in this idea, "the fascinating thing to me is the way the group has a soul, a drive, an intent, an end, a method, a reaction and a set of tropisms which in no way resembles the same things possessed by the men who make up the group. These groups have always been considered as individuals multiplied. And they are not so. They are beings in themselves, entities."

The two ideas, non-teleological thinking and the phalanx, have long been thought to be the product of Steinbeck's association with Ed Ricketts, but they have also been viewed as irreconcilable ideas both in *Sea of Cortez* and in Steinbeck's fiction. The amoral passivity of "is" thinking and the possibility for beneficial and self-directed group action by the phalanx ap-pear to be incompatible, and "is" thinking in particular seems to be foreign to the moral indignation present in much of Steinbeck's fiction of the decade. But with the recent publication of Richard Astro's *John Steinbeck and Edward F. Ricketts: The Shaping of a Novelist* and Elaine Steinbeck and Robert Wallsten's *Steinbeck: A Life in Letters* it can be seen that the problem in fact does not exist. Although both Steinbeck's and Ricketts's names appear on the title page of *Sea of Cortez,* it was always believed that Steinbeck himself wrote the narrative portion of the book and that he therefore assumed full responsibility for all of the ideas in that portion. We now know, however, that Steinbeck incorporated verbatim sections from Ricketts's unpublished philosophical writing including the passage on non-teleological thinking. Although Steinbeck occasionally used or referred to Ricketts's non-teleo-logical beliefs, he was absorbed most of all during the 1930s, as his letters reveal, by the phalanx idea. He could thus either ignore or contradict "is" thinking when other, more compelling beliefs attracted him. In *Sea of Cortez,* for example, the narrator of the voyage (here presumably Steinbeck) records his anger at the Japanese factory fishing boats which were depleting the waters off lower California and thus causing hardship among the Mex-icans. And so in *The Grapes of Wrath* itself Casy's early defense of non-teleological thinking—"There ain't no sin and there ain't no virtue. There's just stuff people do"—is clearly in the context of an attack on a puritan sexual morality. The issue of the anomaly of Steinbeck's non-teleological philosophy is really a nonissue. The concept was largely Ricketts's, and though Steinbeck does occasionally endorse it in special contexts, his own deepest involvement was in the emotionally and morally compelling social activism implied by the phalanx idea.

Thus, there indeed are primitivist, Marxist, Christian, and scientific elements in *The Grapes of Wrath*. But no one of them is the single most dominant element and none is present in a single and obvious way. Rather, they exist in a fabric of complex interrelationship which constitutes both the power and permanence of *The Grapes of Wrath* as a naturalistic tragedy.

The first two portions of *The Grapes of Wrath*—the Joads in Oklahoma and on the road to California—enforce upon us the realization that the more we come to know and admire the humanity of the Joads the more inhumanely they are treated. Steinbeck's success in involving us in this irony derives in part from his ability to place the Joads within two interrelated mythic sources of value: they are primitives and they are folk. Their "natural" ways and feelings touch upon a core belief which in various forms runs through American life from the Enlightenment to the primitivistic faith of such moderns as Faulkner and Hemingway.

The Joads are close to the natural processes and rhythms of life. They are farmers who have always farmed and hunted. They have little education and little association with town or city. Their unit of social life is the family with its "natural" crests of birth, puberty, and marriage at one end of life and aging and death at the other. Indeed, the Joads seem to live in a pretribal stage of social evolution, since their principal contacts are with other families rather than with school, church, or state. Spoken and written expression to them is always a barrier; they communicate largely by action and by an instinctive sensitivity to unspoken feelings. We first encounter them not in person but rather in the long series of anecdotes about them which Tom and Casy share at the opening of the novel, anecdotes which establish their shrewdness, openness, and understanding in a context of crudity and occasional bestiality. But even this texture of animality in their lives helps establish their naturalness.

As primitives, the Joads have an "honest" relationship to their land. They farm to live, not for profit, and out of the intrinsic relationship between their work and their existence there emerges the life-sustaining values of industry and pride as well as an instinctive generosity and compassion. They seem at first lawless because of their opposition to those who wish to remove them from their land, but their experiences on the road reveal that regulation and order in their lives arise organically out of their needs and conditions. The different families meeting each night in makeshift camps along Route 66 quickly establish unwritten codes of behavior which maintain order and equity in the camps.

The care with which Steinbeck molds our sense of the primitive strength of the Joads early in the novel is especially revealed in two areas of their experience. The Joads are attuned to solving the problems of their lives without outside aid. They raise and prepare their own food, they make their own clothes, and they create and maintain their own special form of transportation. We thus come to accept that the Joads are latter-day pioneers, that the myth of the self-sustaining pioneer family still lives in them. But the Joads not only solve problems by the exercise of individual skills but also by the maintenance of a group strength and efficiency. Here Steinbeck is at pains to dramatize his phalanx notion of the distinctive identity of the group. So, for example, in the family councils just before departure or soon after Grandpa's death, the family when it meets to solve its problems becomes a powerful and cohesive single body, "an organization of the unconscious. They obeyed impulses which registered only faintly in their thinking minds."

The Joads are folk as well as primitives; that is, we also experience the comic and the ritualized in their naturalness. For example, the three generations of the Joads constitute a gallery of family folk types: earthy and querulous grandparents, eccentric and even occasionally demented uncles and brothers, cocky and sexually vibrant late adolescents, and overcurious and problem-creating children. Above all, the Joads contain the archetypal center of the folk family, the mother as source of love, wisdom, and strength. The Joads as folk salt the novel with the sexuality and excrementality of folk humor and with the ritualized forms of folk life, particularly of courtship and death. Some of the folk attributes and experiences of the Joads have both a Dickensian predictability of repetitive motif and a freakish humor characteristic of Erskine Caldwell's portrayal of poor whites. (The Joads' discovery of the flush toilet is pure Caldwell.) But the folk element in the lives of the Joads, when combined with the central strain of their primitivism, contributes to rather than diminishes our sense of their basic humanity. The earthiness and humor of the Joads as folk permit Steinbeck to avoid the heavy breathing and lush primitivism of his early fiction—notably of *To a God Unknown*—and encourage us to respond to them not only as symbols but as "real" people.

The Joads as primitive folk appear to be opposed by the life-denying forces of the mechanical, institutional, and intellectual. In Oklahoma these forces are allegorized by the banks and corporations which have the law and wealth on their side but which lack the human attributes of understanding and compassion. The forces are symbolized above all by the impersonal mechanical tractor which destroys the farmers' homes and by the anonymous car which attempts to run over the turtle as it goes about its "business" of spreading the seed of life. Yet the mechanical and the commercial are not inherently evil. The Joads' jerry-built truck soon becomes a symbol of family unity as well as a means of fulfilling their striving for a better life. And the small businessmen along the road and the small California ranchers are themselves threatened with destruction. If the tractor were owned and used by the Joads, Steinbeck tells us, it would be a beneficial mechanical force. The real evils in the Joads' life are thus not the abstractions of the mechanical or the institutional but the human failings of fear, anger, and selfishness. Those who cheat or beleaguer or harass the Joads in Oklahoma and on the road and in California may symbolize the opposition of the structured in life to the natural but they are above all greedy or frightened men who wish to preserve or add to what they own. Steinbeck's depiction of this essentially human conflict suggests that his attempt in *The Grapes of Wrath* was not to dramatize a labored and conventional primitivistic ethic. It was rather to engage us, within the context of primitivistic values, in one of the permanent centers of human experience, that of the difficulty of transcending our own selves and thereby recognizing the nature and needs of others.

Although the Joads as a family are the matrix of this growth, the process of transcendence occurs most pointedly and fully in the lives of Tom, Ma, and Casy. The experiences of these characters illustrate Steinbeck's faith in the ability of man to move from what he calls an "I" to a "we" consciousness. The "conversion" of Tom, Ma, and Casy to a "we" state of mind is both the theme and the form of *The Grapes of Wrath*; it is also Steinbeck's contribution both to the naturalistic theme of the humanity of all sorts and conditions of men and to the naturalistic tragic novel of the 1930s.

Tom is initially the symbol of "natural man." He is big and rawboned, is uncomfortable in store-bought clothes, and he can roll a cigarette or skin a rabbit expertly. He has humor, understanding, and a commonsense shrewdness and he is proud and independent. He judges men and events with generosity of spirit, but his faith in his judgment and in a natural order in life has been tempered by his imprisonment for killing a man in self-defense during a drunken brawl. He cannot understand his punishment and emerges from prison with the belief that it is better to live from moment to moment than to seek to understand and thus to plan.

If Tom is natural man, Ma is natural woman in the roles of wife and mother. Steinbeck's initial description of her renders with a blatantly exultant religiosity her character and function as preserver of the family:

> Her full face was not soft; it was controlled, kindly. Her hazel
> eyes seemed to have experienced all possible tragedy and to have

mounted pain and suffering like steps into a high calm and a superhuman understanding. She seemed to know, to accept, to welcome her position, the citadel of the family, the strong place that could not be taken. . . . And from her great and humble position in the family, she had taken dignity and a clean calm beauty. . . . She seemed to know that if she swayed the family shook, and if she ever really deeply wavered or despaired the family would fall, the family will to function would be gone.

Tom's power lies in his pride and shrewdness, Ma's in her capacity to love and in her sense of continuity. To her, life is not a series of beginnings and endings but rather "all one flow, like a stream, little eddies, little waterfalls. . . . Woman looks at it like that. We ain't gonna die out. People is goin' on—changin' a little, maybe, but goin' right on." If Tom represents natural strength, Ma represents natural religion. She is appalled by the religion of fear and sin which she encounters in the woman in black at Grandma's death and in the "Jesus-lover" at Weedpatch. Her religion is of love, and love to her means constant rededication to preserving the family, just as Tom's strength means solving the problems which this pledge demands.

Whereas Tom and Ma are fully realized both as characters and as symbols, Casy functions principally as a symbol. Dissatisfied with conventional religious truth because it runs counter to his own impulses, he seeks to find God in his own spirit rather than in Bible or church. On the morning of the Joads' departure, he is asked to say grace before breakfast. He seizes the opportunity to tell them of his attempt to commune with God in the hills. He felt a oneness with all things, he explains,

> "An' I got thinkin', on'y it wasn't thinkin', it was deeper down than thinkin'. I got thinkin' how we was holy when we was one thing, an' mankin' was holy when it was one thing. An' it on'y got unholy when one mis'able little fella got the bit in his teeth an' run off his own way, kickin' and draggin' an' fightin'. Fella like that bust the holiness. But when they're all workin' together, not one fella for another fella, but one fella kind of harnessed to the whole shebang—that's right, that's holy."

The Joads, however, scarcely listen; they are absorbed in the expectation of breakfast. And Casy does not really understand the implications of his insight into the nature of "holiness" as a kind of phalanx of group oneness.

The journey of the Joads, and particularly of Tom, Ma, and Casy, is thus not so much to California as toward a full understanding and acceptance of this vision of human sanctity and strength.

The "I" quality of life, man's selfishness in its various forms, is the dominant force in the Oklahoma portion of *The Grapes of Wrath*. It exists not only in the corporate "I" of the banks and land companies which are displacing the Joads but in the Joads themselves. Their intense and instinctive commitment to family unity and preservation is a superficially attractive but nevertheless narrow and limited form of self-absorption. It has already been revealed as ineffective in that it has not prevented their eviction. And the local young man who is driving the tractor which is bulldozing their home displays its vital flaw when he says, in defense of his turning against his own people, "You got no call to worry about anybody's kids but your own." Not to worry about someone else's children, however, as the novel makes clear in incident after incident involving a child, is to aid not only in the destruction of the children of others but of one's own.

The Oklahoma section of the novel also contains several strains of "we" thinking, strains which emerge more clearly and fully as the novel proceeds. The famous description of the turtle crossing the road is a parable not only of persistence within nature—of the turtle continuing his journey with ingenuity and strength despite hazards and setbacks—but of the relatedness and unity of all life. The turtle unconsciously carries in a crevice of his shell a seed from a plant he has brushed against; he thus has both a specific goal and the general function of contributing to the perpetuation of other forms of life. Tom and Ma at this point are somewhat like the turtle in that while pursuing a specific narrow goal they also reveal in several ways an unconscious acceptance of a "we" ethic. Ma, when she reflects on the number of tenant farmers being evicted, moves instinctively toward a Marxist idea of unity: "They say there's a hun'erd thousand of us shoved out. If we was all mad the same way . . . —they wouldn't hunt nobody down." And Tom accepts without question Muley's observation that "If a fella's got somepin to eat an' another fella's hungry—why, the first fella ain't got no choice." But these "we" qualities, like those of the turtle and other animals, are both instinctive and ungeneralized. They have not taken on the human qualities of consciousness and abstraction, the qualities which Steinbeck later in the novel associates with "Manself"—the distinctive ability of man to give up something material, even life itself, for a concept. The "we" in man, though an attribute of the universal potential for a phalanx identity, is distinguished by conscious awareness and direction.

The tension between the primitive folk "I-ness" of the Joads' commitment to family and their tentative reaching out toward a "we-ness" continues on the road. Now, however, new conditions and experiences impress on the Joads a greater sense of the meaning and validity of "we." "I-ness" is of course still paramount in their minds, particularly after Grandpa's death raises the specter of eventual dispersal of the family. Their response to the crisis of his death—the decision to bury him by the side of the road—renews a pioneer custom and thus affirms the primacy of the family in the westering experience. But on the road the Joads encounter families like them in intent and need, such as the Wilsons, and so begin to move out of their isolation. And in the wayside camps the Joads begin to realize the benefits of group cooperation. Perhaps most of all they begin to sense the potential strength in the fact that so many share the same condition; they are beginning to shape in their minds the vital difference, as Steinbeck expresses it in an interchapter, between "I lost my land" and "we lost *our* land."

The California experiences of the Joads—and particularly of Ma and Tom—make explicit to them the difference between "I" and "we." This portion of the novel is divided into four segments. The first two (the Hooverville and Weedpatch) demonstrate concretely to the Joads the opposition between the "I" and "we" ways of life; the second two (the peach ranch and the boxcar) demand of them a conscious allegiance either to "I" or "we." The Hooverville and the government camp at Weedpatch represent, as many readers have complained, a loaded contrast in human values. The Hooverville is an allegorical representation of anarchistic animality, of the anger, cruelty, and desperation of men seeking to survive in a world in which they are pitted against each other. Put in Marxist terms, the Hooverville is a free market economy when the supply of labor exceeds demand and when labor is unorganized. The government camp, though it is an island in a hostile sea, is maintained on the principle of the surrender of some individual rights for the greater good of the whole. Its method is organization to achieve group aims, and its operative unit is the committee. Put in Marxist terms, it is the proletarian state.

The Joads are almost immediately involved in the destructive violence of the Hooverville; at Weedpatch they flourish and contribute to the suppression of violence. As throughout the novel, the ethical distinction between the "I" of the Hooverville and the "we" of Weedpatch is revealed by the treatment of children at the two camps. When the Joads arrive at the Hooverville Ma prepares supper and soon finds herself surrounded by starving children. She is torn between her commitment to her own family and her responsiveness to the silently begging children, and can only cry out, "I dunno what to do. I got to feed the fambly. What'm I gonna do with these here?" In Weedpatch the problem of hungry children is resolved not by depriving one's own—not by the "I" principle of the conflict between mine and yours—but by maintaining a camp fund which dispenses loans to those in need.

The peach ranch to which the Joads are forced to move in order to get work unites the Hooverville and Weedpatch principles in one volatile setting. Inside the ranch, in a kind of prison, are the families driven to the "I" of scabbing because of their desperate need; outside are striking migrants who have organized to help all migrants. Casy had been separated from the Joads at the Hooverville when he had been arrested for coming to the aid of a man being framed by the deputies. He now reappears as a strike leader and union organizer, and explains his conversion to Tom. "Here's me, been a-goin' into the wilderness like Jesus to try to find out somepin. Almost got her sometimes, too, But it's in the jailhouse I really got her." What he had learned in prison, in the incident of the men acting in unison to gain better food, was the principle of group action to achieve just ends. Life had a holy unity both in the wilderness and in jail, but he has discovered in jail that his function was not passively to accept this holiness but to seek actively to render it concrete in social life. Tom, however, doesn't fully understand Casy's explanation, and Casy says, "Maybe I can't tell you. . . . Maybe you got to find out."

The vigilantes attack the strikers, and as Casy is about to be clubbed down, he says, "You fellas don' know what you're doin'. You're helpin' to starve kids." The first sentence of this speech (and its repetition by Casy just before his death) is often cited as a specific parallel between Casy and Christ. In fact, Casy is a Christ figure only in the social-activist sense of the Christian life in *The Grapes of Wrath*. The vigilantes are not killing the son of God but children who have been denied their humanity, and Casy is not sacrificed to vouchsafe a heaven for man but to aid man to achieve a better life on earth. Holiness is not a condition between God (or his son) and man but between man and man, between all the members of the "whole shebang," as Casy put it earlier. Helping to starve children is thus unholy or parallel to killing Christ; helping to create a society in which children will be fed is man's true Christ-like role on earth.

Even though Tom fails to grasp Casy's meaning at this point, he has been growing in understanding. True, his two acts of involvement so far—his coming to the aid of the Hooverville migrant earlier and of Casy now—were instinctive responses to blatant acts of bullying. But he has also been absorbing a sense of the social injustice and of the fundamental inhumanity in the condition of the migrants which is now reaching the level of consciousness. He realizes that the landowners wish not only to employ the migrants but to turn them into a kind of obedient domestic animal. "They're a-workin' away at our spirits," he tells the family. "They're a-tryin' to make us cringe an' crawl like a whipped bitch. They tryin' to break us."

In defending Casy, Tom has killed a man and therefore has to live in the fields when the family moves on to pick cotton and live in an abandoned boxcar. Musing over Casy's ideas and experiences, he now accepts what he had earlier neither understood nor had even consciously heard. Casy, he recalls,

> went out in the wilderness to find his own soul, an' he foun' he
> didn' have no soul that was his'n. Says he foun' he jus' got a
> little piece of a great big soul. Says a wilderness ain't no good,
> 'cause his little piece of a soul wasn't no good 'less it was with
> the rest, an' was whole. Funny how I remember. Didn' think I
> was even listenin'. But I know now a fella ain't no good alone.

Tom here expresses both Casy's wilderness vision and his later social expansion and application of that vision. The wilderness (contemplation and passivity) is not a true joining of one's soul to that of all men; only in social unity and action can this be achieved. So Tom decides to pursue a true "we-ness"; like Casy, he will now attempt to organize the migrants.

The Joads, and particularly Ma, move in an analogous direction. In the crisis of Rose's delivery during the flood, the Wainwrights, who are as beleaguered as the Joads, come to their aid. When Ma tries to thank Mrs. Wainwright, she replies,

> "No need to thank. Ever'body's in the same wagon. S'pose
> we was down. You'd a give us a han'."
> "Yes," Ma said, "we would."
> "Or anybody."
> "Or anybody. Use' ta be the fambly was fust. It ain't so now.
> It's anybody. Worse off we get, the more we got to do."

So Ma, the staunchest defender of the "I" of the family, has come to accept consciously the principle of "we" embodied in the "anybody" of those in need.

The conclusion of the novel, when Rose of Sharon gives her breast to the starving man in the barn, unites in one symbolic act various themes which have been fully dramatized in the conversions of Tom and Ma. Throughout the novel Rose's pregnancy has represented one of the major strands in the primitive character of the Joads as a family. Her childbearing is honored because it is a contribution to family continuity, and it constitutes, because of her intense self-preoccupation, the inward-turning nature of the family. But with the birth of her stillborn child—a child who is the last "starving kid" of the novel—she is freed from these "I" roles. Encouraged by Ma, she can now—in a climactic gesture of conversion—move outward to the "we" of the starving man. She is saying, in effect, that all those who hunger are her children, just as Tom has given himself to the anonymous migrants who require leadership and Ma to the "anybody" who needs.

By the close of the novel the Joads have been stripped clean in several senses. They have lost most of their possessions, including the truck which had served since their departure from Oklahoma as a symbol of family unity. In the family itself, the weak (Grandpa and Grandma) and the irredeemably self-preoccupied (Noah, Connie, and finally Al) have fallen away. Left is a core of Ma and Pa, Uncle John and Rose, and the two children, Ruth and Winfield. With the exception of the children but including Tom, this is a group in which each figure has conformed to the biblical promise that to lose all is often to gain one's salvation; that is, each has struggled through to a form of "we" consciousness. Tom in his decision to trade a day-to-day existence for militant organizing, Ma in her acceptance at last of commitments beyond that of saving the family, Rose in the translation of her biological self-absorption into an almost blissful giving, Pa in his neglect of his anger at his loss of status in the family as he marshals the boxcar migrants into a group effort to save their dwellings, and even John, in that for once his lifelong preoccupation with his guilt is replaced by an outward-directed anger (it is he who sets Rose's dead baby afloat in a box to remind the nearby townspeople that they are starving children)— each has made the journey from "I" to "we."

In one of the major ironic motifs of *The Grapes of Wrath,* this reduction of the Joads to an almost animal struggle for survival also bares fully their essential humanity, their Manself. Throughout the novel the migrants' poverty has been viewed by others as an index of their inhumanity. The gas station attendant at Needles cries, "Them goddamn Okies got no sense and no feeling. They ain't human. A human being wouldn't live like they do. A human being couldn't stand it to be so dirty and miserable." But it is the very absence of that which defines humanity to the limited understanding which at last helps shape the penetrating clarity of spiritual insight of the Joads and thus enables them to discover a transcending sense of oneness with all men.

Our understanding of and response to the Joads' journey to awareness are aided by a number of fictional devices. Of these, the natural and biblical symbolism requires little detailed discussion. The one serves to establish certain similarities between the Joads and natural life, the other between them and man's spiritual character. Together they contribute to Steinbeck's theme of the enriching unity of all life, in which the natural is also the spiritual and the spiritual is also the natural. Less obvious in their function are the interchapters and the cyclic structure of the novel. Both serve as forms of editorial commentary through which the Joads' experience is translated into a statement on the human condition. The interchapters have a number of forms, from generalized narrative and prose poem to dramatic exchange and authorial philosophizing. They also vary in content from social realism to expressionistic exaggeration and in tone from humor and satire to bombast and supplication. But they are bound together, whatever their form, content, or tone, by the underlying authorial emotion of anger. Steinbeck uses the narrative of the Joads to involve us in the tragic pathos of the life of a migrant family, and the interchapters to involve us in the anger we must feel when we understand the inhumanity to man which their lives illustrate. The interchapters not only allegorize the Joads into universal figures of the poor and downtrodden but also engage us, through Steinbeck's devices in these sections, in an intensity of emotion usually foreign to allegory and other forms of abstraction. The interchapters are not extraneous to the novel but rather are central to its ability to move us.

Anger, yet an anger which contains an element of hope, is also an important characteristic of the cyclic form of *The Grapes of Wrath*. The novel begins with the Joads poor and landless in a drought-stricken Oklahoma; it ends with them even poorer and still landless in a flooded California. In Oklahoma, the men are at first silent and puzzled but then become "hard and angry and resistant" as they sit "thinking—figuring." In California, the men, in a parallel moment, are at first fearful and then angry. Anger is thus a source of both strength and continuity. In California, moreover, anger has found a focus and therefore a potential resolution. Nature, whether drought or flood, is not to blame for the condition of the migrants, nor is the Oklahoma tractor driver or the California deputy or ranch foreman. To blame is the greed exemplified by the economic system, and against this force, the Joads, who have thought and figured, have begun to find an answer in their willingness (as symbolized by Tom) to mold themselves into a group force equal in strength. So the last two chapters of the novel end with images of renewal in the midst of the carnage. After the starvation of the winter, "Tiny points of grass came through the earth, and in a few days the hills were pale green with the beginning year"; and after the Joads are driven from the boxcar by the flood, Rose nurses the starving man in the barn.

Much that is central in *The Grapes of Wrath* as a naturalistic novel of the 1930s can be understood by noting the remarkable number of similarities, as well as some significant differences, between it and an earlier naturalistic novel of social conflict in California, Frank Norris's *The Octopus*. In both works a struggle for land occurs within a cycle of natural growth, and in both the weaker figures in the conflict—the wheat ranchers and the migrants—suffer a tragic defeat. But in both instances, the most insightful and feeling of those crushed—Annixter, Vanamee, and Presley, and Tom, Ma, and Casy—struggle through to an understanding both of the underlying nature of the conflict and the essential nature of life. The three young men in *The Octopus* learn that the machinations of men cannot affect the omnipotence and benevolence of the natural process of growth, and the Joads learn to accept the oneness of all existence. Both works are fundamentally naturalistic despite these religious overtones. As is also true of *The Octopus*, the naturalism of *The Grapes of Wrath* resides in the theme that man can find in verifiable natural and social life the basic truths he should live by. In *The Octopus* the continuity of life is discovered not in the Pauline symbol of the seed—that man shall be reborn in heaven—but in the real seed, that man and nature reproduce themselves. And in *The Grapes of Wrath*, Casy's discovery that all things are united in holiness is only a vaguely felt concept until its meaning is completed by his finding that oneness is union organization and that holiness is the power to correct injustice. Men may come to know these truths initially by an instinctive or intuitive reaching out, but the truth itself must be not only felt but also observed and validated in experience. Both novels are thus conversion allegories, but the "religion" to which the characters are converted is that of the sanctity of life itself rather than of some aspect of man, God, or nature which is different from or superior to the life we lead and know.

The Grapes of Wrath also has its own distinctive character as a naturalistic novel of the 1930s. *The Octopus* proclaims that "all things, surely, inevitably, resistlessly work together for good," since the natural process of growth is both omnipotent and beneficent. Although the railroad monopoly is a bad thing which affects individuals adversely, it does not adversely affect mankind in general, since society and its conflicts are subsumed under the cosmic beneficence of the natural order. Men have died in the struggle for a crop of wheat, but the wheat itself will feed the starving millions of India. Steinbeck's perspective is quite different. Much of the fruit grown by the

San Joaquin ranchers doesn't reach anyone because it is destroyed to maintain high prices, an act which aids the wealthy but harms the poor, including the migrant children who hunger for the oranges they see all around them. Steinbeck views the American economic system not as part of a natural process but as a baneful social illustration of the "I" principle. Men can and must struggle through to a "we" activism of camp committees and unions rather than accept that good will eventually accrue to the greatest number through cosmic beneficence. Although Steinbeck in *The Grapes of Wrath* occasionally appears to be endorsing a Marxist theory of historical necessity by his references to the inevitability of class conflict if class divisions continue to grow, he is really endorsing a naturalistic version of a traditional social gospel activism in which one's beliefs must be realized in social life as well as be expressed in the temple.

Some of the obvious and often noted defects of *The Grapes of Wrath* stem from its character as a 1930s naturalistic novel, though a good many of these are less disturbing if the allegorical mode of the novel is at once accepted. Parables such as the turtle crossing the road, characters who exist principally as symbols, the hell-paradise contrast of the Hooverville and Weedpatch—these are major weaknesses only if one adopts the notion that naturalism is limited to the probabilities of social realism. Much more significant as a flaw in *The Grapes of Wrath* is the conflict between its tragic and social impulses. Steinbeck asks us to respond to the fate of the Joads with the compassion we bring to other accounts of men who must be stripped naked and suffer before they can understand the needs of the poor naked wretches around them. But he also generates intense anger toward those causing the misery of the Joads and points out ways in which their condition can be improved. The two intents seem to be related. It is the economic system as a whole which is the equivalent of the Joads' initial "I" values. Thus, compassion for their suffering as they move toward a "we" consciousness, and anger at the economic system for failing to undergo this change appear to be coordinate sentiments. But in fact the presence of these two emotions both diffuses and confuses the tragic theme and form of the novel. Steinbeck has succeeded so well in engaging us in the nature and quality of the Joads as primitive folk that the family assumes a validity at odds with his ultimate goal for them. We wish the Joads to find a better life in California, but we are not really persuaded that the committees and unions and other activities which represent the "we" principle in their lives are really better than the folk inwardness and the clearly definable entity that is their family. Here we are perhaps victims of a change in perspective since the 1930s in that we are no longer convinced that committees are inherently superior to other forms of awareness and action. We are also reacting in a way unforeseen by Steinbeck to his conviction that the humblest man can rise to the wisest thoughts. Steinbeck believed that it would be primarily the "thoughts"—the acceptance by the Joads of "we-ness"—which would hold us. But instead it is the Joads themselves who are the source of the enduring power of the novel.

Steinbeck and Nature's Self: *The Grapes of Wrath*

John J. Conder

Both Dreiser and Dos Passos saw the self as a product of mechanisms and hence incapable of freedom, and both postulated the existence of a second self beyond the limitations of determinism. Dreiser arrived late at the notion and, borrowing it wholesale from Brahmanic thought, barely tested its meaning, save to see it as the source of man's freedom. Although Dos Passos never developed a version of such a self, he early found its existence and suppression the cause of man's misery and, in elaborating on that theme, he was able to enlarge a cluster of themes and attitudes associated with a second self—in particular those associated with its relationship to society and to nature. In *The Grapes of Wrath*, Steinbeck renders his version of a second self in man and brings to mature development that cluster of themes and attitudes. Significantly, he brings them to maturity within a framework of determinism and so harmonizes authentic freedom and determinism in a way that Dos Passos never could do, since the second self, the true source of man's freedom, remains forever an embryo in his pages.

The interchapters of Steinbeck's novel create a network of interlocking determinisms through their emphasis on the operations of abstract, impersonal forces in the lives of the Oklahomans. Chapter 5 is especially effective both in capturing the poignancy of the human situation created by such forces and in pointing to the kind of deterministic force underlying the others in the novel. In one fleeting episode a nameless Oklahoman who threatens the driver of a bulldozer leveling his house is told that armed

From *Naturalism in American Fiction: The Classic Phase.* © 1984 by the University Press of Kentucky.

resistance is futile, for the driver acts in the service of the bank, and "the bank gets orders from the East." The Oklahoman cries, "But where does it stop? Who can we shoot?" "I don't know," the driver replies. "Maybe there's nobody to shoot. Maybe the thing isn't men at all. Maybe . . . the property's doing it." Or at least the Bank, the monster requiring "profits all the time" in order to live and dwarfing in size and power even the owner men, who feel "caught in something larger than themselves."

The vision that appears here has a name: economic determinism. This view does not say that man has no free will. One might indeed find among a group of bank presidents a corporate Thoreau who prefers jail (or unemployment) to following the demands of the system. It merely asserts that most men charged with the operation of an economic structure will act according to rules requiring the bank's dispossession of its debtors when a disaster renders them incapable of meeting payments on their mortgaged property. Far from denying free will, such determinism fully expects and provides for the willed resistance of the Oklahomans. The police take care of that. Nor is this vision without its moral component, though neither the police nor the owner men can be held individually responsible. "Some of the owner men were kind," Steinbeck writes, "because they hated what they had to do, and some of them were angry because they hated to be cruel, and some of them were cold because they had long ago found that one could not be an owner unless one were cold." These anonymous men are not devil figures but individuals performing functions within a system, so the work indicts the system rather than individuals who act in its service. In the case of the Oklahomans, the indictment is founded on a fundamental irony: societies, designed to protect men from nature's destructive features—here a drought—complete nature's destructive work, expelling men from the dust bowl into which nature's drought has temporarily transformed their farms.

But the expulsion of the Oklahomans is not the only inexorable consequence of the operation of economic force. These men, women, and children who "clustered like bugs near to shelter and to water" automatically create in their camps a society within the larger society, acting according to the same instinctual dictate that initially made the Joad family, seeking self-preservation, seem "a part of an organization of the unconscious." "Although no one told them," the families instinctively learned "what rights are monstrous and must be destroyed"—the "rights" of rape, adultery, and the like—and which must be preserved. Instinct welds the group "to one thing, one unit"; and the contempt, fear, and hostility they encounter as they traveled the highways "like ants and searched for work, for food" reinforce the bonds of group solidarity by releasing an anger whose ferment "changed them . . . united them" all the more. Here is the basis of that much-remarked-on shift in the novel from farmer to migrant, from "I" to "we," from family to group.

This emphasis upon the spontaneous development of a social group is not limited to the interchapters; but it is there that Steinbeck notes not only the inevitability of its development but, more important, the concurrent emergence of a group consciousness and the inevitable future consequences that its emergence entails. Economic determinism thus spawns responses that are biologically determined. Of course the scope of Steinbeck's biological determinism is sharply limited. He states with certainty but two simple facts: that the "anlage of movement" possessed by the oatbeards, foxtails, and clover burrs of chapter 3 has its counterpart in the anlage of "two squatting men" discussing their common plight, and that the realization of the potential in such anlage is inevitable. As the narrative voice proclaims to the owner men: "Here is the anlage of the thing you fear. This is the zygote. For here 'I lost my land' is changed; a cell is split and from its splitting grows the thing you hate—'*We* lost *our* land.' " Thus, forces that destroy one community create another by stimulating the communal anlage inherent in instinct, which sets the primary goals of life—in the Oklahomans' case, survival.

→ But in a novel that so beautifully portrays society as a system of interrelated forces, there is more to the matter than what has just been described. If economic determinism breeds biological determinism, biological determinism in turn spawns an inevitable social conflict that in time becomes an historically determined sequence of events with predictable outcome. Although there are references to it elsewhere, chapter 19 most clearly transforms this economic determinism into an historical one. It describes armed Californians, who earlier had stolen land from Mexicans, guarding the stolen land. Following the pattern of the Romans ("although they did not know it"), "they imported slaves, although they did not call them slaves: Chinese, Japanese, Mexicans, Filipinos." Later appear the dispossessed Oklahomans of the East, "like ants scurrying for work, for food, and most of all for land." When the slaves rebel, Steinbeck, using repetition, emphasizes the cause-effect relationship between the migrants' condition and their rebellion against it. "The great owners, striking at the immediate thing, the widening government, the growing labor unity; . . . not knowing these things are results, not causes. Results, not causes; results, not causes. The causes lie deep and simply." And that he believes these causes compel the appearance of the effect proceeding from them—that is, believes the causes determine that effect's emergence—becomes clear in chapter 19 when he associates "the inevitability of the day" when the owners must lose their land with their violent temporizing: "Only means to destroy revolt were considered, while the causes of revolt went on."

But now some observations about the relation of the interchapters and the plot of *The Grapes of Wrath* are needed in order to show that Steinbeck's determinism can embrace freedom of the will because his literary structure creates a statistical determinism. The interchapters display the growth of a group consciousness controlled by instinct's response to the dynamic of economic forces. This emphasis is carried into the story in a variety of ways, most notably through Ma's insistence on keeping the family together. But in the story proper, instinct does not rule each person with equal power. The instinctual power that drives the group in the interchapters is unequally distributed among its individual members. Granpa's resistance to leaving Oklahoma testifies to the power of age to overcome the instinct to survive. And age is not the only force limiting the role of instinct in individual lives. Attached to his land, Muley Graves refuses to leave it in order to depart for California. He makes a choice that reduces him to "a ol' graveyard ghos' " living by night as a trespasser on land once his own. Noah finds the hardships of the journey greater than the comfort derived from the group and leaves, last seen walking by a river into the greenery of the surrounding countryside to an unknown future. Connie, angry that he did not remain to work for the bank (and thus aid in the Oklahomans' dispossession), abandons his pregnant wife Rosasharn.

In the plot, then, free will plays a major role. Even those who remain with the group make numerous free choices to assure its survival, as Ma's words about the need to get to California testify: "It ain't kin we? It's will we?" This emphasis on choice and free will sets limits on the rule of instinct, limits that avoid reducing the individual to the level of a will-less animal, a mere pawn of instinct. Man's possession of instinct roots him in nature, but he is different from other things in nature, as Steinbeck makes clear by describing in chapter 14 man's willingness to "die for a concept" as the "one quality [that] is the foundation of Manself . . . distinctive in the universe." And this emphasis on man's uniqueness in nature, so inextricably related to his will, in turn limits the scope of the novel's historical determinism, which is based on Steinbeck's biological determinism. Even in the group that will give history its future shape, there are individuals who will depart from the historical patterns which that group is aborning.

Seen in this way, Steinbeck's determinism does not at first sight seem a far cry from Dos Passos's, at least insofar as the economic base that underlies their respective deterministic outlooks issues in a statistical determinism for each writer. But Steinbeck's interchapters are a technical innovation that create a significant expansion and difference of vision, first appearances notwithstanding. Steinbeck gains two major advantages from them. First, by creating this preserve for rendering abstract social forces, he releases a considerable number of other chapters—his plot chapters— for portraying characters as developing states of consciousness rather than as those fragments of force which they seem to be in *Manhattan Transfer*. He thereby can *emphasize* the existence of free will in his novel. Just by making freely willed decisions the basis of his statistical determinism, in other words, he gives will a role more prominent than the one it plays in Dos Passos's work, where chance prevails and will is nugatory.

The second advantage is of far greater importance because it shows Steinbeck's idiosyncratic way of harmonizing determinism and freedom. In addition to portraying abstract forces operating on a grand scale in space and time, those chapters also are instrumental in showing the change in the group from an organism biologically determined by instinct and externally determined by social forces to an organism that achieves rationality and hence a freedom of will capable of transcending the bonds of determinism. The interchapters are indispensable because they dramatize Steinbeck's belief that a group is a living organism possessing a life of its own independent of the individuals who comprise it, and the implementation of that view is a part of the novel's genius.

Steinbeck clarifies his view of a group in *Sea of Cortez,* a collaboration of sorts, where in a passage specifically written by him he uses marine analogies to explain his sense of the normal relation of an individual to the group of which he is a part:

> There are colonies of pelagic tunicates which have taken a shape
> like the fingers of a glove. Each member of the colony is an
> individual animal, but the colony is another individual animal,
> not at all like the sum of its individuals. Some of the colonists,
> girdling the open end, have developed the ability, one against
> the other, of making a pulsing movement very like muscular
> action. Others of the colonists collect the food and distribute it,
> and the outside of the glove is hardened and protected against
> contact. Here are two animals, and yet the same thing. . . . So
> a man of individualistic reason, if he must ask, "Which is the
> animal, the colony or the individual?" must abandon his partic-
> ular kind of reason and say, "Why, it's two animals and they

aren't alike any more than the cells of my body are like me. I am much more than the sum of my cells and, for all I know, they are much more than the division of me." There is no question in such acceptance, but rather the basis for a far deeper understanding of us and our world.

This quotation stresses the individuality of the group and the uniqueness, apart from it, of its component elements. In the following quotation Steinbeck introduces an added dimension in the larger animal, here a school of fish:

And this larger animal, the school, seems to have a nature and drive and ends of its own. . . . If we can think in this way, it will not seem so unbelievable . . . that it seems to be directed by a school intelligence. . . . We suspect that when the school is studied as an animal rather than as a sum of unit fish, it will be found that certain units are assigned special functions to perform; that weaker or slower units may even take their place as placating food for the predators for the sake of the security of the school as an animal.

Biology thus seems to confirm the eternal copresence of the one and the many. Applying the thrust of the thought of this passage to the relation of the human individual to his group, one can account for this phenomenon, the purposiveness of the larger animal independent of the individuals composing it, only by assuming that individual men have a dual nature, both a group identity and a personal one independent of it but not necessarily in conflict with it.

More must be made of this observation, but in order to do so precisely, it is necessary to restate the earlier relation established between interchapters and plot, using now not the language of determinism and free will but language taken from Steinbeck's quotation above. The content of the interchapters and the content of the plot of *The Grapes of Wrath* relate to each other as the larger animal (the migrant group) to the individuals composing it. The plot portrays members of the school in their rich individuality, whereas the interchapters show the formation of the larger animal that they compose, a formation that takes place both on a de facto level (by virtue of circumstance, a physical group is formed) and on an instinctive one, which endows the animal with life. By virtue of the instinct for self-preservation, in the camps twenty families become one large family, sharing a single instinct. The animal can come to life on this instinctual level because the animal's anlage is in the separate family, the basic unit through which man fulfills his needs, and the instinctual sense of unity is strengthened by a common set of threatening circumstances issuing in shared emotions: first fear, then anger. In this condition, the "school intelligence" directing its drives is instinctual alone, and hence the human group is more like the school of fish to which Steinbeck refers. Guided solely by instinct, the human group-animal achieves a measure of protection from a hostile social environment, but with instinct alone, it can no more transcend the social determinism of the body politic than the turtle (which in the novel symbolizes it in this condition) can transcend the machinations of the drivers eager to squash it. Chance alone can save the group or the turtle as both walk, like Tom, one step ahead of the other, living from day to day.

But the group changes, and in this respect the plot goes one step further than the interchapters, which halt with the fermenting of the grapes of wrath. For the plot shows the emergence of a rational group consciousness, first in Casy, then in Tom, whose final talk with his mother, representing the principle of family, discloses that his own consciousness has transcended such limitations. In fact it is mainly in Tom that the group develops a head for its body; for he survives the murdered Casy, and he was from the beginning more clearly a member of the de facto group than Casy, who owned no land. And by stressing how the animal that is the group achieves rational consciousness and (hence) freedom, Steinbeck harmonizes freedom and determinism in his most important way. The group determined by instinct and circumstance in the interchapters achieves both rational self-awareness and freedom in the person of a member who substitutes the consciousness of a group for a private consciousness and thus gives the group access to the faculty of human will. Tom thus enables it to move from instinct to reason and to that freedom which reasoned acts of the will provide. By having the group consciousness mature in the plot section of his novel, Steinbeck thus unites it to the interchapters structurally and harmonizes his novel philosophically.

And he provides a triumph for the group within the context of determinism, for their attainment of rational group consciousness is itself a determined event because such potential is inherent in the species. Their achieved freedom of will as a group thus is the final term of a socially determined sequence of events that leads to the group's creation, and the group's exercise of it to attain its ends fulfills the historical determinism of the novel. Yet this is not the only hope in these pages, for the prospective triumph of the group provides hope for the triumph of the individual as a whole person.

The Grapes of Wrath is the story of the exploitation of a dispossessed group, and it is difficult not feel that it will always engender sympathies for the dispossessed of the earth wherever and whenever they might appear. But the novel's indictment of society for what it does to individuals should have an equally enduring appeal; for here its message goes beyond the conditions of oppressed groups and addresses individuals in all strata of complex societies. The condition of individual Oklahomans in fact is an extreme representation of the condition of social man, and in the capacity of individual Oklahomans to change lies the hope for social man.

The migrants' achievement of rational freedom speaks for more than freedom for the group. It tells readers of a vital difference in kinds of freedom. Steinbeck has written, "I believe that man is a double thing—a group animal and at the same time an individual. And it occurs to me that he cannot successfully be the second until he has fulfilled the first." Only the fulfilled group self can create a successful personal self; only freedom exercised by a personal self in harmony with a group self can be significant.

This aspect of the novel's vision depends upon Steinbeck's fuller conception of an individual's two selves. One is his social self, definable by the role he plays in society and by the attitudes he has imbibed from its major institutions. The other is what is best called his species self. It contains all the biological mechanisms—his need for sexual expression, for example—that link him to other creatures in nature. And by virtue of the fact that he is thus linked to the natural world, he can feel a sense of unity with it in its inanimate as well as its animate forms. But the biological element in this self also connects him to the world of man, for it gives him an instinctive sense of identification with other members of his species, just as the members of other species have an instinctive sense of oneness with their own kind.

The species self thus has connections to nonhuman and human nature, and Steinbeck refers to the latter connection when he speaks of man as a "group animal." He views a healthy personal identity as one in which the species self in both its aspects can express itself through the social self of the individual. But society thwarts, or seeks to thwart, the expression of that self. It seeks not only to cut man off from his awareness of his connections to nonhuman nature, it seeks also to sever him from the group sense of oneness with the human species that the individual's species self possesses. Ironically, therefore, purely social man loses a sense of that unity with others which society presumably exists to promote.

The novel's social criticism rests on this view, and its emphasis on grotesques, purely social beings cut off from their connections to nature, both human and nonhuman, portrays an all-too-familiar image of modern man. In too many instances, by imposing mechanical rhythms on human nature, society creates half-men. Its repeated attempts to distort the individual's identity is emphasized by numerous dichotomies between social demands and instinct. Tom tries to comprehend the meaning of his imprisonment for killing in self-defense. Casy tries to understand the meaning of his preaching sexual abstinence when he cannot remain chaste himself. And the point is made by the basic events that set the story moving. A mechanical monster, indifferent to the maternal instincts of the Ma Joads who exercise their species selves in the interest of family solidarity, expels families from their land. The social mechanism thus tries to thwart the demands of the group aspect of the self to remain together. And the same mechanism is responsible for sowing what has become a dust bowl with cotton, rendering it permanently useless for agriculture, thus showing its indifference—nay, hostility—to the connections with nature that the species self feels.

This suppression of the species self is not rigorously foreordained for every individual, and hence the novel's determinism does not rest on the universality of its occurrence. Ma's personality remains undistorted from the novel's beginning to its end. Her intense commitment to the family proceeds from a very live species self; and though she must enlarge her vision to include more than her family, her insistence that Casy join the family on its westward exodus and numerous demonstrations of her concern for others outside her immediate family bear witness that her vision is not all that limited to begin with. But such suppression is nonetheless widespread, and indeed a sufficient number of people must be transformed into grotesques if social structures are to perpetuate themselves. They thereby make many men grotesques and subject all men to economic determinism. Thus the attention to grotesques is part of the pattern of economic determinism in the novel; such determinism can only prevail under conditions guaranteeing with statistical certainty that society can distort man's nature.

The novel singles out two social institutions that assure the creation of grotesques: religion and the law. Lizbeth Sandry is the major representative of a grotesque created by religion. Her intolerance of dancing represents her intolerance of sex, and such intolerance displays religion's warping influence on human instinct. She arouses Ma's ire by warning Rosasharn, "If you got sin on you—you better watch out for that there baby." Her religious views, importing a supernatural mandate into the realm of nature, impose on natural behavior value judgments (like "sin") designed to thwart the normal expression of the species self. This divorce

between her social and species selves, indicated by her views, makes Lizbeth
Sandry much like one of Sherwood Anderson's grotesques, as all social
selves alienated from the species self must be.

Uncle John and Connie's wife, Rosasharn, carry into the family Lizbeth
Sandry's fanaticism. Uncle John's felt sense of guilt over his wife's death
impels him to blame all the family misfortunes on what he takes to be his
sin: his failure to summon a doctor when she complained of physical ail-
ments. His exaggerated sense of sin fails to take into account his own human
nature (his natural fallibility) and circumstance; for his reluctance to call a
doctor doubtlessly depended on strained finances. His compulsive references
to that sin make him as much a grotesque as Lizbeth Sandry, his grotesquerie
compounded by his need for wild drinking bouts to escape the sin.

Not only does he become a grotesque, but his obsession with sin blinds
Uncle John to the true cause of the family's misfortunes and so shows that
religion can indeed be an opiate of the people useful for sustaining an unjust
social structure. In this sense Rosasharn is like him, for she has been affected
by Lizbeth Sandry's sense of sin. Of course, Rosasharn's sense of sin does
not transform her into the grotesque that Uncle John has become. It illustrates that selfishness noted by other critics, for throughout most of the
novel she thinks only of herself and her unborn baby, to the total exclusion
of the problems of other people. But her view of Tom's killing a deputy,
which is one illustration of her selfishness (she shows concern only for her
baby, not for her brother), also points to the larger consequences of Uncle
John's obsession with sin. She tells Tom, "That lady tol' me. She says what
sin's gonna do. . . . An' now you kill a fella. What chance that baby got
to get bore right?" Like Uncle John's explanation for family misfortunes,
her view of the real-enough threat to her unborn child deflects the source
of that threat into a theological realm inaccessible to man, the realm of the
devil who tempts man's fallen nature to sin, rather than assigning it to the
realm of the accessible and the real, the social forces responsible for
the deaths of Casy, the deputy, and her own child.

If religion enforces a split between man's two selves, suppressing one
and thus deforming the other, so do most social institutions. Hence the law
motif is central to the novel, law being the second (and more important)
institution that Steinbeck indicts in his defense of the self; for it is law that
holds society's other institutions together and, supported by police power,
gives them their governing authority.

References to the law appear in a variety of contexts, but their meaning
is best embodied in the opposition between law and fundamental human
needs, those "got to's" to which Casy refers that compel men to say,

"They's lots a things 'gainst the law that we can't he'p doin'." Burying Granpa, for example, in defiance of local edict. But there are more important illustrations of how the law thwarts the expression of man's nature, even when it does not manage to distort it. Tom finds no meaning, at the novel's outset, in a system that imprisons him for killing in self-defense, and he discovers the true meaning of the system only after he kills the deputy who murders Casy—a nice bit of symmetry that illustrates his growth in awareness as he perceives, like Casy, that his second killing is also an instinctual response, one of self-defense against the true assaulter, the system, which so thwarts man's instinctual life that it leaves him no choice other than to strike back. This line of meaning is echoed by others: by Ma, who says of Purty Boy Floyd, "He wan't a bad boy. Jus' got drove in a corner"; by the nameless owner men who tell the tenants early in the novel, "You'll be stealing if you try to stay, you'll be murderous if you kill to stay." And it is implicit in Tom's own position at the beginning of the plot: to leave the state violates the conditions of his parole, yet to stay means to break up the family and to face unemployment and possible starvation.

Under such circumstances, it is not surprising to discover that the true prison in *The Grapes of Wrath* is the world outside the prison walls, the real point of Tom's story of a man who deliberately violated parole to return to jail so that he could enjoy the "conveniences" (among them good food) so conspicuously absent in his home. "Here's me, been a-goin' into the wilderness like Jesus to try to find out somepin," Casy says. "Almost got her sometimes, too. But it's in the jail house I really got her." He discovers his proper relationship to men there because it is the place of the free: of men who exercised the natural rights of nature's self only to be imprisoned by the society that resents their exercise. And in fact he can see how the law violates self because he has already seen how religion does. Without the revelations of the wilderness, he would not have had the revelation of the jailhouse; the first is indispensable to the second. Together, they make him the touchstone for understanding the novel's philosophy of self and for measuring the selves of the novel's other characters.

Just as the species self is the ultimate source of freedom for a group, it is the same for an individual. If man can recognize that he is a part of nature by virtue of that self's existence—if he can affirm for this aspect of a naturalistic vision—he can liberate himself from the condition of being a grotesque and, in recognizing his oneness with others, escape the tentacles of economic determinism as well. This is the novel's philosophy of self, and Casy's life is its lived example, both in his thought and in his practice.

Casy has arrived at the vision that man is a part of nature in the novel's opening pages, the discrepancy between his religious preachment and his sexual practice prompting his withdrawal from society to go to the hills in order to comprehend his true relation to the world and leading to his Emersonian sense of connection with nonhuman nature: " 'There was the hills, an' there was me, an' we wasn't separate no more.' " Casy has thus found his deepest nature, that self which is connected even to nonhuman nature, and so he has taken the first vital step toward his liberation. In his way of recovering this self, Casy should be measured less by Emerson than by Thoreau, who went to the woods "to drive life into a corner" and discovered that "not till we are lost . . . , not till we have lost the world, do we begin to find ourselves, and realize where we are and the infinite extent of our relations." For Thoreau, as for Casy and Steinbeck, a true knowledge of the relationship between one's self and the external world can only be derived from an empirical study of the structure of physical reality. Such empiricism imparts the knowledge that man does relate to the whole and inspires, in Steinbeck's words written elsewhere, "the feeling we call religious," the sense of unity between self and outside world that makes "a Jesus, a St. Augustine, a St. Francis, a Roger Bacon, a Charles Darwin, and an Einstein." Writing of his own interest "in relationships of animal to animal," Steinbeck later gave a clue to the general source of the religious vision at which Casy has arrived at the beginning of *The Grapes of Wrath:*

> If one observes in this relational sense, it seems apparent that species are only commas in a sentence, that each species is at once the point and the base of a pyramid, that all life is relational to the point where an Einsteinian relativity seems to emerge. And then not only the meaning but the feeling about species grows misty. One merges into another, groups melt into eco-logical groups until the time when what we know as life meets and enters what we think of as non-life: barnacle and rock, rock and earth, earth and tree, tree and rain and air. And the units nestle into the whole and are inseparable from it.
>
> *(Sea of Cortez)*

Any reader of "Song of Myself" would know instantly what Casy and Steinbeck mean. This sense of relationship inspires reverence not for an unknowable God outside of nature but for knowable nature in all its forms; for if one feels united to "the hills," one is clearly in a position to take the next step and feel reverence for nature in its animate forms, and especially in the form known as the human species to which all men belong.

And Casy has clearly taken this step as well, as his subsequent remarks on the holiness of man testify. "I got thinkin' how we was holy when we was one thing, an' mankin' was holy when it was one thing." Such human holiness and the consequent sense of human solidarity it engenders come from each man feeling he is "kind of harnessed to the whole shebang," to all of nature. In finding his deepest self, then, Casy has run against the grain of his old social self to embrace a naturalistic religious view which, from Steinbeck's angle of vision, more surely inspires that sense of brotherly love preached by Christianity than Christianity does. A passage from *The Log from the Sea of Cortez* aptly represents the religious view of the novel:

> Why do we so dread to think of our species as a species? Can it be that we are afraid of what we may find? That human self-love would suffer too much and that the image of God might prove to be a mask? This could be only partly true, for if we could cease to wear the image of a kindly, bearded, interstellar dictator, we might find ourselves true images of his kingdom, our eyes the nebulae, and universes in our cells.

By descending into his species self, Casy abandons the arrogance of social man who thinks of himself only in terms of his distinctiveness in nature. Specifically, he abandons his social self as preacher and the limitations which it imposes on creating significant relationships with the world outside. As a preacher he necessarily divorced himself from his species self, with its instinctual need for sexual expression, because of Christianity's sexual ethic. Or, rather, since in fact he did act on these instincts, it is more accurate to say that the Christian sexual ethic cut him off from the knowledge that his species self is his better self. Not only does it promote a sense of connection with nature which a Christian sense of man's uniqueness denies—more important, it promotes a sense of connections with all of mankind suppressed by Christianity's parochialism, its division of the world between those who possess the truth and those who live in outer darkness.

Casy's reverence for nature (which also inspires a reverence for human life) allows him to escape character deformations visible in other figures in the novel. Such reverence is markedly absent in men who use their cars to try to run a turtle down, just as it is absent in Al, who swerves his car to squash a snake. When Al becomes "the soul of the car," of course, he is helping his family in their and his time of need, and to that extent the promptings of his species self are very much with him. But its larger sympathies are blunted because the social means by which he is forced to help his family, the automobile on which he must rely, tarnishes him with the taint of "mechanical man," a phrase Steinbeck uses to describe the social man divorced from his species self, and thus accounts for his squashing the snake. In the car he loses contact with that aspect of the species self which reveres life in all its forms, and by so much he becomes a warped victim of society.

Casy escapes this kind of warping because he has established a relationship to the whole, to nonhuman nature. But he also escapes the warping of an Uncle John or a Lizbeth Sandry because he is empirical in establishing a relation to the parts, to the members of the human community which must be man's first concern, as he makes clear when he says, "I ain't gonna preach" and "I ain't gonna baptize":

> "I'm gonna work in the fiel's, in the green fiel's an' I'm gonna
> be near to folks. I ain't gonna try to teach 'em nothin'. I'm
> gonna try to learn. Gonna learn why the folks walks in the grass,
> gonna hear 'em talk, gonna hear 'em sing. Gonna listen to kids
> eatin' mush. Gonna hear husban' an' wife a-poundin' the mat-
> tress in the night. Gonna eat with 'em an' learn. . . . All that's
> holy, all that's what I didn' understan'. All them things is the
> good things."

Like Thoreau, Casy has reason to believe that most men "have *somewhat hastily* concluded that it is the chief end of man here to 'glorify God and enjoy him forever.' " But his empiricism, not oddly at all, makes him accept in others the very religious view he has already rejected, for such might prove to be the true expression of another's nature. Here he is best measured by Emerson, the Emerson who proclaimed, "Obey thyself," when he tells Uncle John, "I know this—a man got to do what he got to do," or when he says of Uncle John's obsession: "For anybody else it was a mistake, but if you think it was a sin—then it's a sin."

And he follows Emerson in another way. Casy's interest in the parts shows that, like Emerson, he cannot rest satisfied with a religious "high," the feeling of oneness with "the all" that he has already experienced at the novel's opening and that Emerson experienced as "a transparent eyeball." Like Emerson, he must translate the insight derived from that experience into ethical terms on the level of practical action. Having concluded that the devil whom most men should fear is society ("they's somepin worse'n the devil got hold a the country"), he not surprisingly discovers the level of practical action by which he can relate to them in a prison, whose inmates are there mainly " 'cause they stole stuff; an' mostly it was stuff they needed an' couldn' get no other way. . . . It's need that makes all the trouble."

Since society cannot provide man's basic needs, Casy will help to secure them and, in the process, he brings his species self into relation with men by adopting a social one that permits its expression. He becomes a strike organizer.

Casy's new personal identity is thus an expression of a larger self which, as Emerson knew, can be realized in a diverse number of concrete social forms, though such self-realization earns the world's displeasure. Members of the family who remain in the group thus move toward that larger self when they abandon older views of theological sin as a causal factor in human affairs and approximate Casy's newer view in their words and actions. Uncle John displays this movement, his escape from the ranks of the grotesque, when he floats Rosasharn's stillborn baby to the town, admonishing it to "go down in the street an' rot an' tell 'em that way," just as Rosasharn does when she breastfeeds the old man in the novel's closing paragraph. Her gesture acknowledges the truth of Uncle John's words, that the sin that killed her baby was social and not theological in origin. The same gesture shows her overcoming a solipsism engendered by her pregnancy by enlarging the sympathies of her species self to embrace more than the child that society denied her. That gesture, finally, is the perfect one to signal the awakening of nature's self, the self growing from that human biological nature which mothers and fathers the species.

The novel thus suggests the desirability of a society based not on absolutes imported supernaturally into nature by systems derived from a priori thinking, but one whose institutions accommodate themselves to subjective absolutes. In this way Steinbeck's novel expands the naturalistic vision of *Manhattan Transfer*. It develops the theme only subordinate in the earlier novel: man and nature are one, not two. But *The Grapes of Wrath* is also a logical and satisfying conclusion to naturalism prior to Dos Passos. If man's connections to nonhuman nature seemed a source of savagery for Crane, nonetheless, at the last, nature in "The Open Boat" was just nature— a vast system for man to interpret for his own benefit, could he but escape the complicated social fabric to see that the primary purpose of societies is to aid him in creating such interpretations. Even in *McTeague*, brute nature is not entirely without its redeeming values: it alone provides McTeague with the sixth sense to flee the city that so twists the lives of the people in Norris's pages. Because the novel is so completely deterministic, however, nature is not used as an avenue of escape. In its form as sexual drive, it instead contributes to McTeague's destruction. But for Steinbeck, nature did become a viable avenue of escape when he developed a religious vision based on the feeling resulting from empirically ascertainable knowledge, the knowledge that man is related to the vast system called Nature. This vision is implicit in Dreiser's view of a creative spirit, but unlike Dreiser, Steinbeck postulates no unknowable purpose in this spirit possibly running at cross-purposes to man's own. He escapes the tentacles of determinism that hold Dreiser's men and women in thrall because he does not unravel the Hobbesian dilemma; because he does not reduce consciousness to temperament or instinct; because he instead makes consciousness in the service of man's instinct the center of man's freedom. Like Emerson, and Dreiser at the last, he assumes that if nature's spirit has purpose, man as part of it can give it expression and direction by realizing his own purpose. To attain knowledge of this ability is to begin to meet the demands of spring.

The Indestructible Women: Ma Joad and Rose of Sharon

Mimi Reisel Gladstein

The three authors discussed in this [essay] may be similar in some ways, but obviously there are more differences than similarities in their works. Because of these differences they project their conceptions about the indestructible woman in widely varying ways. There are no female characters in Steinbeck who match the lush sensuality of the goddesslike Eula Varner or who are wounded fighting in foreign wars as Linda Snopes was; nor is there a Steinbeck heroine with the worldly sophistication and pizzazz to match Brett Ashley's or the unusual maturity of the 19-year-old Renata. Faulkner's women are limited regionally; they are all Southerners. The majority of Hemingway's significant heroines are continentals or Americans living or working abroad. Steinbeck's female characters come from a variety of geographical locations in the United States and Mexico. While geography is not necessarily a sound basis for literary differentiation, in the case of these three authors it is important because setting plays such an important part in their themes. More significantly, since all are primitivists, albeit of differing orthodoxy, the land functions as a positive value in all of their works. Where the various indestructible women are described in terms of nature imagery, or where they function as earth goddess types, there is a correlation in the ways that Faulkner, Hemingway, and Steinbeck portray them. That is perhaps the only similarity in the way these three men depict the indestructible woman.

John Ditsky suggests that there are certain parallels in Faulkner's and

From *The Indestructible Woman in Faulkner, Hemingway, and Steinbeck.* © 1974, 1986 by Mimi Reisel Gladstein. UMI Research Press, 1986.

Steinbeck's treatment of nature in relation to character, but that there are more outstanding differences, the basic difference being that Faulkner is consistent in his use of attitude toward the land as a criterion for judging human worth, while Steinbeck is not. Faulkner's "basically agrarian principles" dominate his thinking from his earliest works through his Nobel Prize address. "Furthermore," explains Ditsky, "there is a strong possibility that serious differences emerged from Steinbeck's evident desire never to write the same type of book twice, while Faulkner saw himself as trying repeatedly to get one book written successfully." Perhaps the fact that Faulkner lived on the land and saw himself as a farmer contributed to his consistent concern with and attitude toward the land. Though Steinbeck did some farm work as a boy and young man, his movement when he started writing was in an urban direction; he launched his married life in Pacific Grove and later lived in New York City. Since Faulkner's works embody a criterion that judges people by their coherence with natural processes, women, as closely attuned to these processes, are seen as enduring. Some of Steinbeck's women fall into a similar classification.

Faulkner works in one setting inhabited by a variety of character types; Hemingway uses one predominant plot pattern and protagonist type. When discussing Steinbeck's works, however, most critics stress the diversity of both technique and subject matter. Nevertheless there are certain consistencies in his works. Lester Jay Marks in his thoughtful evaluation of thematic design in Steinbeck's novels suggests three recurring thematic patterns. One of these patterns proposes that humankind may be viewed biologically, as a "group animal" composed of individuals ("cells") but having a will and intelligence of its own, distinct from any one of its parts. Most of the enduring women in Steinbeck derive their positive value from the fact that they act as the nurturing and reproductive machinery of the group. Their optimistic significance lies, not in their individual spiritual triumph, but in their function as perpetuators of the species. They are not judged by any biblical or traditional sense of morality. The Hemingway credo may maintain that immorality was what made you feel disgusted afterward; the Steinbeck credo reads that perhaps there is no such thing as sin, only how people are. Those people who act for the good of the group or the greatest number, in whatever manner, are those whose behavior is valued. A number of Steinbeck's indestructible women function within that ethical construct.

During the writing of this [essay], I was asked by students and colleagues about the subject of my research. The reply that I was analyzing a character type which I had chosen to call the indestructible woman in the works of Faulkner, Hemingway, and Steinbeck brought forth a standard response. "Well, there is Ma Joad, but who else?" Ma Joad is perhaps the most easily recognizable example of the type. Her characterization is so unabashedly representative of these writers' attitude toward the indestructibility of woman that were it not for the fact that she follows rather than precedes others of her type in their works, she might be called the archetype of the breed in American fiction.

In terms of overwhelming odds, both physical and mental, none of the other characters covered in this study has quite as much to endure as Ma Joad. The novel begins with her being uprooted from her home, having her center of being capsized. When he son Tom comments on the resultant change in her character, she explains, "I never had my house pushed over . . . I never had my fambly stuck out on the road. I never had to sell—ever'thing." Not only is her home destroyed, but she must, because of the limited space in the truck, burn her mementos, her relics of the past. This she does of her own accord, privately, and without letting the others see the pain it causes her.

After losing her home and the tokens of the past, Ma must endure a series of deaths and hardships. First Grandpa does not survive the uprooting. Ma's compassion is displayed during Grandma's illness as Ma strives to make her comfortable, fanning Grandma, tending to her. Then Grandma succumbs. Ma's behavior on the occasion of Grandma's death is illustrative of her great compassion and personal indomitability. Ma also acts to impart to Rose of Sharon the need for responsibility and sharing, encouraging her daughter to fan Grandma also during her final illness. Because Ma is aware of the family need for her as a citadel of strength, she cannot even openly display her anguish. "Rose of Sharon watched her secretly. And when she saw Ma fighting with her face, Rose of Sharon closed her eyes and pretended to be asleep." Ma is so thoroughly dedicated to the good of the greater number that she lies all night with Grandma's dead body in her arms until the group gets across the state border and the California desert. The toll of this deed shows: "Her face was stiff and putty-like, and her eyes seemed to have sunk deep into her head, and the rims were red with weariness." Even after the family has made it across and Ma tells them why she did what she did, she does not break down. As Tom moves to comfort her, she says, "Don't touch me. . . . I'll hol' up if you don't touch me. That'd get me."

All those in contact with her are aware of Ma's awesome indestructibility. "The family looked at Ma with a little terror at her strength." Casey assesses the enormity of Ma's deed: "All night long, an' she was alone. Johnny there's a woman so great with love—she scares me. Makes me afraid an' mean."

Grandma's death is only the beginning of the trial Ma has to face. More deaths and departures follow. Noah decides to desert the group. The Wilsons must be left behind; Connie leaves. Casey is killed and Tom becomes a fugitive. Rose of Sharon's baby is born dead. All around them there is starvation and deprivation, harassment and hostility. To add to these disasters a flood forces what's left of the family to abandon their camp. Through all this Ma remains strong and steadfast.

Ma Joad stands out in Steinbeck's works as a complete and positive characterization of a woman. Few of his other women are so fully drawn. None of his other women functions on so many interpretive levels, all affirmative. Not only is Ma realistically characterized as a believable woman, but she is also the embodiment of the myth of the pioneer woman, the symbol for positive motherhood, and the earth goddess incarnate. In a writer whose works are criticized for their preponderance of misfits, aberrations, and cripples, the characterization of Ma Joad's strength and goodness is a positive statement about the quality possible in the female.

Throughout the novel, Ma Joad functions as a nurturing mother to all. The fact that she is known only as "Ma" and is not given a first name reinforces her maternal image. The reader is first introduced to her while she is preparing food for the family, the traditional job of the mother. Not only does she prepare food for her own family, but she also welcomes strangers and offers to share with them whatever she has. She has baked bread, the staff of life, and symbolically she is the provider of both life and its sustenance. The image is of Mother Earth or Lady Bountiful. Her description emphasizes her maternal role. "Ma was heavy, but not fat; thick with child-bearing and work. She wore a loose Mother Hubbard of gray cloth in which there had once been colored flowers."

Ma mothers not only her biological children, but any and all who are in need of care. She even mothers Grandma and Grandpa, chasing Grandpa down to button his pants as if he were a little boy, seeing to Grandma's needs. Her Mother Earth image is strongly reinforced by the scene where she feeds the starving children who gather around her kettle. Though there is not enough to feed her family adequately, she ladles small portions so as to leave some for the children. In every situation in the novel, Ma is ready to share whatever she has with those in need; her way of being is mothering.

In the scenes of Ma chasing down Grandpa or suffering because she does not have enough to provide for both her family and the hungry children in the camp, Ma is dramatically depicted in a realistic way. However,

Steinbeck, who explained in a letter to his editor Pascal Covici that the novel had five layers, acquaints readers with Ma's archetypal role very early in the story. His initial description of her stresses her superhuman qualities. She is called "the citadel of the family, the strong place that could not be taken." Her position as wise and healing goddess also makes her the family judge. Her reaction to all this distances her from the ordinary mortals in the family. She becomes an ideal; everyone looks to her for guidance. Her affirmative and indestructible qualities are accentuated:

> Her hazel eyes seemed to have experienced all possible tragedy and to have mounted pain and suffering like steps into a high calm and a superhuman understanding. She seemed to know, to accept, to welcome her position. . . . And since old Tom and the children could not know hurt or fear unless she acknowledged hurt and fear, she had practised denying them in herself. And since, when a joyful thing happened, they looked to see whether joy was on her, it was her habit to build up laughter out of inadequate materials. But better than joy was the calm. Imperturbability could be depended upon. And from her great and humble position in the family she had taken dignity and a clean calm beauty. From her position as healer, her hands had grown sure and cool and quiet; from her position as arbiter she had become as remote and faultless in judgment as a goddess.

Ma knows that she is the foundation of the family; they stand or fall on the basis of her strength. Steinbeck makes that clear.

But Ma's characterization transcends the mythic, as mythic characters tend to be flat and static. Her characterization, both narrative and dramatic, is multidimensional. Her character rises from the pages of the book as much more than Mother Earth or serene and aloof goddess. She is both leader and follower, a wise yet ignorant woman, simple in many ways and still complex. Hers is a fully developed realistic portrait, notwithstanding those critics who think she is too good to be true. Her strengths as a person are enhanced because Steinbeck chooses to show us, along with those situations in which she behaves heroically, examples of her weaknesses and doubts.

Although she behaves bravely, Ma also expresses her fears. Her bravery is not of the foolhardy kind where actions arise instinctually without forethought. Ma has the intelligence to be frightened, but to act in spite of her fears. When Al asks her if she is afraid, she responds, "A little . . . Only it ain't like scaired so much. I'm jus' a settin' here waitin'. When somepin happens that I got to do somepin—I'll do it." She also expresses her fear to Tom; in this case it is the fear that his departure will undermine the already weakened family structure. "We're crackin' up, Tom. There ain't no fambly now."

Like any human being she fantasizes about the future, making plans for money that is yet unearned. "I wonder—that is if we all get jobs an' all work—maybe we can get one of them little white houses." In the government camp, uplifted by the sanitary conditions and hospitable reception, Ma dreams of a stove, a tent, and secondhand springs for the bed. Her sights are set progressively lower as fewer and fewer of her initial expectations are met. In the latter part of the novel she expresses her desire for even temporary housing: " 'F we pick plenty peaches we might get a house, pay rent even, for a couple months."

Steinbeck's fully rounded portrait of this indestructible woman includes instances of her ignorance, suspicion, and pride. Having never seen bathroom facilities such as those at the government camp, she inadvertently ends up in the men's room. Her country background and pride make her suspicious of strangers and wary. She rejects the camp manager's friendly overtures until she is sure of his purpose. She is not free of a little family pride, boasting of the Joad lineage, "We're Joads. We don't look up to nobody. Grampa's grampa, he fit in the Revolution. We was farm people till the debt." She is nostalgic about the past, reminiscing with Rose of Sharon about her younger days. "Maybe you wouldn' think it, but your Pa was as nice a dancer as I ever seen, when he was young."

While Hemingway often equates female passivity with the positive indestructible qualities of women, Steinbeck creates a number of indestructible women who are active and assertive. Ma Joad is both. She displays a number of traditionally masculine qualities without losing her womanly image. Pa Joad recounts with pride the story of how Ma "beat the hell out of a tin peddler with a live chicken." The story is humorous, but it serves as a foreshadowing for Ma Joad's future situation.

> "An' Ma ain't nobody you can push aroun' neither. I seen her beat hell out of a tin peddler with a live chicken once 'cause he give her an argument. She had the chicken in one han', an' the ax in the other, about to cut its head off. She aimed to go for that peddler with the ax, but she forgot which hand was which, an' she takes after him with the chicken. Couldn' even eat that chicken when she got done. They wasn't nothing but a pair a legs in her han'."

Though Ma struggles against those forces which are destroying her family, her weapons prove to be as ineffective as a live chicken. She fights with all her might and is left with little more than an inedible pair of chicken legs.

Another scene that emphasizes Ma's forceful qualities is when she challenges Pa with a jack handle. Whereas in Hemingway's stories the female who threatens male authority is a destructive force, in a number of Steinbeck's works women assume the authoritative role for the good of the group. Ma not only challenges patriarchal authority but she does it in a traditionally masculine way, by a challenge to one-to-one combat. When Pa and Tom have decided that the group should split up, Casey and Tom remaining with the Wilsons, Ma balks. "I ain't a-gonna go," she says as she balances the jack handle in her hand.

> And now Ma's mouth set hard. She said softly, "on'y way you gonna get me to go is whup me." She moved the jack handle gently again. "An' I'll shame you Pa. I won't take no whuppin', cryin' an' a-beggin'. I'll light into you. An' you ain't so sure you can whup me anyways. An' if ya do get me, I swear to God I'll wait till you got your back turned, or you're gettin' down, an' I'll knock you belly-up with a bucket, I swear to Holy Jesus' sake I will."

Ma's challenge is made to prevent the weakening of the group structure, not for personal power. The fact that she acts on instinct as an agent for group preservation is underlined by her surprise at what she has done. Once the group realizes that she has taken control, that she is the power, they decide not to try to fight her. Tom reasons that even if he and Pa and the whole group try to rush Ma, it wouldn't do any good and so he says, "You win, Ma. Put away that jack handle 'fore you hurt somebody." At this point, Ma, who has been acting instinctually, comes out of her trance. "Ma looked in astonishment at the bar of iron. Her hand trembled. She dropped her weapon on the ground."

Ma Joad is not the only indestructible woman in *The Grapes of Wrath*. Just as Faulkner used the Demeter/Persephone myth to suggest a pattern of continuity and resurrection in the relationship of mother and daughter, so in his development of Ma Joad and her daughter Rose of Sharon Steinbeck too plays on the theme of the endless renewal of the female principle. Though Levant claims that the final scene of the novel is a disaster because, among other things, "there is no preparation for Rose of Sharon's transformation," all through the story Steinbeck shows us Ma instructing Rose of Sharon and teaching her through precept and example nourishing and reinforcing behavior patterns. Rose of Sharon, who prior to the beginning of the story had been "a plump, passionate hoyden," is changed by her pregnancy. As the child grows within her, and she prepares to convert her role from daughter to mother, she becomes "balanced, careful, wise." Her whole thought and action turn inward and she is consumed with her sense of self as potential mother, as a reproductive agent. At the beginning of the trip to California Connie and Rose of Sharon share a universe of their own: "The world had drawn close around them, and they were the center of it, or rather Rose of Sharon was in the center of it with Connie making a small orbit around her." Harshly, they are blasted out of their selfish cycles. Connie behaves badly, abandoning both the family and group effort as well as his wife and expected child. Rose of Sharon, on the other hand, endures many deprivations and deaths and by the end of the novel is ready to take her place beside Ma as a pillar of the family.

Rose of Sharon prepares for this role in a number of ways. She aids Ma with the care of the dying Grandma. She helps not only with care of the dying but also with nourishing the living. Even when she is feeling very weak as a result of both malnutrition and pregnancy, she tries to help with the cooking and cleaning chores. "I oughta help Ma . . . I tried, but ever' time I stirred about I throwed up." Bedraggled and burdened, deserted by her husband, Rose of Sharon still drags herself out of bed to do her part in earning money for the support of the family. Sick and weak, she insists on participating in the cotton picking. Ma tries to dissuade her, but she is adamant.

> The girl set her jaw. "I'm a-goin'," she said.
> "Ma, I got to go."
> "Well, you got no cotton sack. You can't pull no sack."
> "I'll pick into your sack."
> "I wisht you wouldn'."
> "I'm a-goin'."

Rose of Sharon goes to pick cotton with the family in her weakened state and becomes even more worn out. Her eyes lose their luster. She shivers and her knees buckle, but she holds her head high.

Ma instructs Rose of Sharon about her responsibilities in the cycle of life. She explains the terror, the loneliness, and the joy of woman's lot. In Ma's philosophy the hurt and the pain do not matter because they are part of the continuity of the species. The eternal cycle of womanhood is represented in a scene where Grandma, Ma, and Rose of Sharon are together in a tent: Grandma is dying; Ma is caring for her; Rose of Sharon is pregnant. Ma uses the occasion to prepare Rose of Sharon for what being a woman entails:

> Ma raised her eyes to the girl's face. Ma's eyes were patient, but the lines of strain were on her forehead. . . . "When you're young, Rosasharn, ever'thing that happens is a thing all by itself. It's a lonely thing. I know, I 'member, Rosasharn." Her mouth loved the name of her daughter. "You gonna have a baby, Rosasharn, and that's somepin to you lonely and away. That's gonna hurt you, an' the hurt'll be lonely hurt, an' this tent is alone in the worl', Rosasharn."

But while Ma acknowledges the pain and the loneliness that are in store for Rose of Sharon, she also tries to share with her daughter her ability to transcend those experiences.

> And Ma went on, "They's a time of change, an' when that comes, dyin' is a piece of all dyin', and bearin' is a piece of all bearin', an' bearin' an' dyin' is two pieces of the same thing. An' then things ain't lonely any more, Rosasharn. I wisht I would tell you so you'd know, but I can't." And her voice was so soft, so full of love, that tears crowded into Rose of Sharon's eyes, and flowed over her eyes and blinded her.

Rose of Sharon's tears show that she has been touched by Ma's explanation.

Steinbeck shows us Ma infusing Rose of Sharon with her own strength and indomitability. In two particularly meaningful scenes, Ma symbolically passes the torch to Rose of Sharon. In the first of these scenes, the torch is passed by means of an icon, earrings, an appropriately feminine symbol. In this scene Rose of Sharon is initially shown in a deep depression, moving sluggishly about her work. She has been nibbling on a piece of slack lime because of the lack of calcium in her diet. She is sick, lonely, deserted, and fears the effect of this situation on her unborn child: "Rose of Sharon said dully, 'If Connie hadn' went away, we'd a had a little house by now, with him studyin' an' all. Would a got milk like I need. Would a had a nice baby. This here baby ain't gonna be no good. I ought a had milk.' " To force her out of her lethargy and coax her out of her pessimistic stance, Ma gives her a pair of small gold earrings that are one of the few things she has painfully salvaged from the past. In order to wear the earrings, however, Rose of Sharon must bear the pain of having her ears pierced. Symbolically, she must suffer to prove herself ready to assume Ma's responsibilities and position. Lest we miss the import of this scene, Steinbeck underlines it for us. Rose of Sharon asks, "Does it mean somepin?" Ma answers, "Why, 'course it does . . . 'Course it does."

The final scene in the book is the other significant indicator that Rose of Sharon will succeed Ma as enduring matriarch, indestructible woman. The scene has been problematic for critics. Steinbeck's editor, Pascal Covici, tried in his diplomatic manner to get Steinbeck to rethink it. "No one could fail to be moved by the incident of Rose of Sharon giving her breast to the dying man," wrote Covici, "yet, taken as the finale of such a book with all its vastness and surge, it struck us on reflection as being too abrupt." But Steinbeck would not be swayed. He wanted the scene as it was for a number of reasons: first, he saw the action as "a survival symbol not a love symbol"; second, he did not want the reader to come away from the story satisfied, for he had done his damndest "to rip a reader's nerves to rags." As for the genesis of the action, Steinbeck explained, "The incident of the earth mother feeding by the breast is older than literature."

Response to this scene had been varied. Steinbeck was amazed at how few critics understood it. Martin Shockley sees the scene in terms of Christian theology, suggesting that Rose of Sharon becomes a Christ figure:

> The meaning of this incident, Steinbeck's final paragraph, is clear in terms of Christian symbolism. . . . Rosasharn gives what Christ gave, what we receive in memory of Him. The ultimate mystery of the Christian religion is realized as Rosasharn "Looked up and across the barn, and her lips came together and smiled mysteriously." *This is My body,* says Rosasharn, and becomes the Resurrection and the Life. Rose of Sharon, the life-giver, symbolizes the resurrective aspect of Christ. . . . In her, death and life are one, and through her, life triumphs over death.
>
> ("Christian Symbolism in *The Grapes of Wrath*")

Eric W. Carlson disagrees with any analysis which attempts to cram a stark, primal symbol into the mold of orthodox Christian symbolism and doctrine. He can accept an interpretation which sees Rose of Sharon's act as symbolically transmuting her maternal love into a love of all people. He sees the final scene as "symbolizing the main theme of the novel: the prime function of life is to nourish life." Numerous others have presented their viewpoints on both the significance and the efficacy of this final scene. Howard Levant calls it "the nadir of bad Steinbeck," because of his claim that Steinbeck did not foreshadow the scene, having given the reader no preparation for his "forcing Rose of Sharon into an unprepared and purely formalistic role." My previous argument should illustrate that Steinbeck did prepare the reader for Rose of Sharon's assumption of Ma's mantle. But whether the critic thinks that the scene is one of tawdry fake symbolism, symbolic of the Eucharist, representative of the rapprochement with the transcendental oversoul, or in keeping with ancient analogies of the behavior of virtuous women, they are all in agreement that the scene has optimistic and positive implications.

Two things in the scene argue strongly for an interpretation that includes Rose of Sharon among Steinbeck's indestructible women. First, Rose of Sharon has become an extension of Ma. As in the Demeter/Persephone myth, the daughter has become the mother. Having experienced great pain, she has been forged as Ma has, through suffering. A parity between the two women has been established. Up until this point in the novel, Rose of Sharon is always referred to as a girl, but in the narrative description of this final scene, Steinbeck emphasizes the equal status of the pair: "and the two women looked deep into each other." In the bulk of the novel, Ma has been the nourisher, the one who sees to the feeding of family and strangers. In this scene, though Ma is the instigator, she cannot do the feeding. It must be Rose of Sharon. By giving her breast to the old man, Rose of Sharon takes her place with Ma as earth goddess. Her youth and fertility combine with her selfless act to signify continuity and hope.

The second idea that should be stressed here is the sex of Steinbeck's symbols of hope and fortitude, Ma Joad and Rose of Sharon. Throughout the novel Steinbeck emphasizes the special indestructibility of women. When the men are disheartened and defeated, the women bear up and take charge. Pa comments on this phenomenon twice. As the family is mired in the comfort of the Weedpatch camp, it is Ma who demands affirmative action. The relative comfort of the camp does not lull her into complacency. She knows that they cannot continue without adequate food or work. "We got to do somepin. . . . You're scairt to talk. An' the money is gone. You're scairt to talk it out. Ever' night you jes' eat, then you get wanderin' away. . . . Now don't none of you get up till we figger somepin out." When the men voice their discouragement, Ma remonstrates, "You ain't got the right to get discouraged. This here fambly's goin' under. You jus' ain't got the right." It is not because she does not feel the same things the men feel, though many critics who cannot accept her strength as realistic ignore the scenes when Ma's vulnerability shows. She never lets her weakness show because she knows the effect that would have on the family. When, after her ordeal with Grandma, Jim Casy says, "She looks tar'd . . . Real tar'd like she's sick—tar'd," she hears his words and immediately reacts. "Slowly her relaxed face tightened, and the lines disappeared from the taut muscular face. Her eyes sharpened and her shoulders straightened."

In the scene where Ma forces the family out of their lethargy, Pa comments, "Time was when a man said what we'd do. Seems like women is tellin' now. Seems like it's purty near time to get out a stick." Ma's reaction to this speech illustrates her special kind of authority, an authority which meets the demands of the time:

> "Times when they's food an' a place to set, then maybe you can use your stick an' keep your skin whole. But you ain't a-doin' your job, either a-thinkin' or a-workin'. If you was, why, you could use your stick, an' women folks'd sniffle their nose an' creep-mouse aroun'. But you just get out a stick now an' you ain't lickin' no woman you're a-fightin', cause I got a stick all laid out too."

In her response to Pa she speaks not only for herself but for all women. The implication of her statement is that women will be subservient in the good times when there is plenty and the men are providing, but that in times of deprivation, a woman's true character, a commanding one, will [come] out. In hard times, women are not only just as tough, but probably tougher than men.

In one of the final scenes of the book, after Ma has had to send Tom away, Mr. Wainwright comes to the family because he is concerned about the possibility that his daughter Aggie may become pregnant. Aggie and Al have been walking out every night and Mr. Wainwright does not want any shame to come to his family. Ma speaks up, assuring Mr. Wainwright that Pa will talk to Al, "Or if Pa won't, I will." Realizing that she has usurped Pa's place, Ma apologizes, but Pa assures her that he realizes that she meant no harm. He is disheartened: "I ain't no good anymore . . . Funny! Women takin' over the fambly. Woman sayin' we'll do this here, an we'll go there. An I don' even care."

Just as Pablo in *For Whom the Bell Tolls* is "terminated," at least temporarily, by the life of the guerrilla band and Pilar takes over as commander of the group, so Pa too is undone by the uprooting of his family and Ma must take over. Leonard Lutwack has noted that Ma Joad, Pilar, and Dilsey all function in similar ways in the novels that they inhabit. In his exploration of the epic tradition in twentieth-century American fiction, he focuses on their roles as mother goddesses inspiring and protecting their hero sons. There are many other similarities between Ma Joad and Pilar. They are certainly two of the most fully drawn of the indestructible women created by these two authors. Why do these women survive when others succumb? Why are they able to command in times of crisis and then turn over the reins of authority to their men when the men can once again cope?

Hemingway does not provide any clues, nor do his characters see the situation as having anything to do with gender. Steinbeck, on the other hand, in both his narration and through his characters proffers generalizations about the differences in the sexes' abilities to cope with change and disaster. Ma, whose wisdom on most matters is respected by both her creator and her family, explains the reason that the women are more enduring than the men. "Woman can change better'n a man," she says. When Pa is ready to give up and sees no hope for the future, Ma articulates her conception of an essential difference between the way men and women handle rites of passage:

> "Man, he lives in jerks—baby born an' a man dies, an that's
> a jerk—gets a farm an' loses his farm, an' that's a jerk. Woman,
> it's all one flow, like a stream, little eddies, little waterfalls, but
> the river, it goes right on. Woman looks at it like that. We ain't
> gonna die out. People is goin' on—changin' a little, maybe, but
> goin' right on."

The analogy between woman and a river is an apt one for this self-characterization by an indestructible woman. Like the river, like the stream of life, she goes on. She is allied to the natural flow of things.

Steinbeck's controversial ending is in keeping with a theme he sounds throughout this novel and in others of his works. In *The Grapes of Wrath* Steinbeck chooses two women to act as his symbols for survival. The objects of their ministrations are two men. Ma Joad and Rose of Sharon in the midst of rain and flood behave in the manner described by Ma as woman's way—like a river, they go right on.

Chronology

1902	John Ernst Steinbeck born February 27 in Salinas, California.
1919	Graduates from Salinas High School.
1920–25	Attends Stanford and works as laborer intermittently. Publishes first short stories in *The Stanford Spectator*.
1925	Drops out of Stanford and goes to New York. Works as construction laborer and reports for the *American*.
1926	Returns to California, writes stories and novels.
1929	*Cup of Gold* published.
1930	Marries Carol Henning and settles in Pacific Grove. Meets Edward F. Ricketts, a marine biologist.
1932	*The Pastures of Heaven*. Moves to Los Angeles.
1933	*To a God Unknown*. Returns to Monterey. *The Red Pony* appears in two parts in *North American Review*.
1934	"The Murder" wins the O. Henry Prize.
1935	*Tortilla Flat* published.
1936	*In Dubious Battle*. Steinbeck travels to Mexico.
1937	*Of Mice and Men*. *The Red Pony* in three parts. Travels to Europe and later from Oklahoma to California with migrants.
1938	*The Long Valley*.
1939	*The Grapes of Wrath*, which wins the Pulitzer Prize.
1940	Sets out with Ricketts to collect marine invertebrates in the Gulf of California.
1941	*Sea of Cortez* published, with Edward F. Ricketts.
1942	*The Moon Is Down*. Steinbeck divorces Carol Henning. *Bombs Away* written for the U.S. Air Force.
1943	Marries Gwendolyn Conger and moves to New York. In Europe covering the war as correspondent for *The New York Herald Tribune*.

1944   Writes script for Alfred Hitchcock's *Lifeboat*. Son Thomas born.

1945   *Cannery Row*. *The Red Pony* with fourth part, "The Leader of the People." "The Pearl of the World" appears in *Women's Home Companion*.

1946   Son John born.

1947   Travels in Russia with photographer Robert Capa. *The Wayward Bus*. *The Pearl*.

1948   *A Russian Journal*. Divorces Gwendolyn Conger. Edward Ricketts is killed in a car-train crash.

1950   *Burning Bright*. Writes script for *Viva Zapata!* Marries Elaine Scott.

1951   *The Log from the Sea of Cortez*, with a preface about Edward Ricketts.

1952   *East of Eden*.

1954   *Sweet Thursday*.

1957   *The Short Reign of Pippin IV*.

1958   *Once There Was a War*, a collection of war dispatches.

1960   Steinbeck takes a three-month tour of America with his dog, Charley.

1961   *The Winter of Our Discontent*.

1962   *Travels with Charley in Search of America*. Wins the Nobel Prize for literature.

1964   Awarded United States Medal of Freedom.

1965   Reports from Vietnam for *Newsday*.

1966   *America and Americans*.

1968   Dies December 20, buried in Salinas.

1969   *Journals of a Novel: The* East of Eden *Letters*.

1976   *The Acts of King Arthur and His Noble Knights*.

Contributors

HAROLD BLOOM, Sterling Professor of the Humanities at Yale University, is the author of *The Anxiety of Influence, Poetry and Repression,* and many other volumes of literary criticism. His forthcoming study, *Freud: Transference and Authority,* attempts a full-scale reading of all of Freud's major writings. A MacArthur Prize Fellow, he is general editor of five series of literary criticism published by Chelsea House. During 1987–88, he served as Charles Eliot Norton Professor of Poetry at Harvard University.

FREDERIC I. CARPENTER taught at the University of Chicago, Harvard University, and the University of California, Berkeley. He is the author of *Emerson Handbook, Emerson and Asia, American Literature and the Dream,* and *The American Myth.*

HOWARD LEVANT is the author of *The Novels of John Steinbeck* and now teaches in the Department of Photographic Arts and Sciences at the Rochester Institute of Technology.

JAMES D. BRASCH teaches English at McMaster University in Ontario and has written on Hemingway.

FLOYD C. WATKINS, Professor of English at Emory University, is the author of *The Flesh and the Word, The Death of Art,* and books on Robert Penn Warren and Thomas Wolfe.

SYLVIA JENKINS COOK teaches English at the University of Missouri and is the author of *From Tobacco Road to Route 66: The Poor White in Fiction.*

DONALD PIZER, Pierce Butler Professor of English at Tulane University, has written extensively on American literary naturalism.

JOHN J. CONDER is Associate Professor of English at Vanderbilt University. He is the author of *Naturalism in American Literature: The Classic Phase.*

Mimi Reisel Gladstein is Associate Professor of English at the University of Texas, El Paso, and the author of *The Indestructible Woman in Faulkner, Hemingway, and Steinbeck.*

Bibliography

Aaron, Daniel. "The Radical Humanism of John Steinbeck: *The Grapes of Wrath* Thirty Years Later." *Saturday Review*, 28 September 1968.

Beach, Joseph Warren. "John Steinbeck: Art and Propaganda." In *American Fiction 1920–1940*, 327–47. New York: Macmillan, 1941.

Benson, Jackson J. "'To Tom, Who Lived It': John Steinbeck and the Man from Weedpatch." *Journal of Modern Literature* 5 (1976): 151–94.

Bluefarb, Sam. "The Joads: Flight into the Social Soul." In *The Escape Motif in the American Novel: Mark Twain to Richard Wright*, 94–112. Columbus: Ohio State University Press, 1972.

Bluestone, George. "*The Grapes of Wrath*." In *Novels into Film*, 147–69. Baltimore: The Johns Hopkins University Press, 1957.

Bowron, Bernard. "*The Grapes of Wrath*: A 'Wagons West' Romance." *Colorado Quarterly* 3, no. 1 (Summer 1954): 84–91.

Browning, Chris. "Grapes Symbolism in *The Grapes of Wrath*." *Discourse* 11 (1968): 129–40.

Carlson, Eric W. "Symbolism in *The Grapes of Wrath*." *College English* 19 (1959): 172–75.

Chametzky, Jules. "The Ambivalent Endings of *The Grapes of Wrath*." *Modern Fiction Studies* 11 (1965): 34–44.

Cox, Martha Heasley. "The Conclusion of *The Grapes of Wrath*: Steinbeck's Concept and Execution." *San Jose Studies* 1, no. 3 (1975): 73–81.

———. "Fact into Fiction in *The Grapes of Wrath*: The Weedpatch and Arvin Camps." In *John Steinbeck: East and West*, edited by Tetsumaro Hayashi, Yasuo Hashiguichi, and Richard F. Peterson, 12–21. Muncie, Ind.: The John Steinbeck Society of America, English Department, Ball State University, 1978.

Crockett, H. Kelly. "The Bible and *The Grapes of Wrath*." *College English* 24 (1962): 193–99.

Davis, Robert Con, ed. *Twentieth Century Interpretations of* The Grapes of Wrath: *A Collection of Critical Essays*. Englewood Cliffs, N.J.: Prentice-Hall, 1982.

Davis, Robert Murray, ed. *Steinbeck: A Collection of Critical Essays*. Englewood Cliffs, N.J.: Prentice-Hall, 1972.

De Lisle, Harold F. "Style and Idea in Steinbeck's 'The Turtle.'" *Style* 4 (Spring 1970): 145–54.

Ditsky, John. "The Ending of *The Grapes of Wrath*: A Further Commentary." *Aqora* 2, no. 2 (Fall 1973): 41–50.

———. "*The Grapes of Wrath:* A Reconsideration." *Southern Humanities Review* 13 (1979): 215–20.

Donohue, Agnes M., ed. *A Casebook on* The Grapes of Wrath. New York: Crowell, 1968.

Eisinger, Chester E. "Jeffersonian Agrarianism in *The Grapes of Wrath*." *University of Kansas City Review* 14 (1947): 149–54.

Emory, Doug. "Point of View and Narrative Voice in *The Grapes of Wrath:* Steinbeck and Ford." In *Narrative Strategies: Original Essays in Film and Prose Fiction,* edited by Syndy M. Conger and Janice R. Welsch, 129–35. Macomb: Western Illinois University, 1980.

Fontenrose, Joseph. "*The Grapes of Wrath*." In *John Steinbeck: An Introduction and Interpretation,* 67–83. New York: Barnes & Noble, 1963.

Fossey, W. Richard. "The End of the Western Dream: *The Grapes of Wrath* and Oklahoma." *Cimarron Review* 22 (1973): 25–34.

French, Warren. *A Companion to* The Grapes of Wrath. New York: Viking, 1963.

———. "*The Grapes of Wrath*." In *A Study Guide to Steinbeck: A Handbook to His Major Works,* edited by Tetsumaro Hayashi, 29–46. Metuchen, N.J.: Scarecrow, 1974.

———. "A Troubled Nation—'How Nice It's Gonna Be, Maybe, in California.'" In *The Social Novel at the End of an Era,* 42–86. Carbondale: Southern Illinois University Press, 1966.

Garcia, Reloy. "The Rocky Road to Eldorado: The Journey Motif in John Steinbeck's *The Grapes of Wrath*." *Steinbeck Quarterly* 14 (1981): 83–93.

Griffin, Robert J., and William A. Freedman. "Machines and Animals: Pervasive Motifs in *The Grapes of Wrath*." *Journal of English and Germanic Philology* 62, no. 3 (July 1963): 569–80.

Hunter, J. Paul. "Steinbeck's Wine of Affirmation in *The Grapes of Wrath*." In *Essays in Modern American Literature,* edited by Richard E. Langford, 76–89. DeLand, Fla.: Stetson University Press, 1963.

Lisca, Peter. "The Dynamics of Continuity in *The Grapes of Wrath*." In *From Irving to Steinbeck: Studies of American Literature in Honor of Harry R. Warfel,* edited by Motley Deakin and Peter Lisca, 127–40. Gainesville: University of Florida Press, 1972.

———. "*The Grapes of Wrath* as Fiction." *PMLA* 72 (1957): 296–309.

———, ed. *The Grapes of Wrath: Text and Criticism.* New York: Viking, 1972.

McCarthy, Paul. "House and Shelter as Symbol in *The Grapes of Wrath*." *South Dakota Review* 5, no. 4 (1967–68): 48–67.

Marks, Lester Jay. "*The Grapes of Wrath*." In *Thematic Design in the Novels of John Steinbeck,* 66–82. The Hague: Mouton, 1969.

Motley, Warren. "From Patriarchy to Matriarchy: Ma Joad's Role in *The Grapes of Wrath*." *American Literature* 54 (1982): 397–412.

Mullen, Patrick B. "American Folklife and *The Grapes of Wrath*." *Journal of American Culture* 1, no. 4 (Winter 1978): 742–53.

Owens, Louis. "*The Grapes of Wrath*: Eden Exposed." In *John Steinbeck's Revision of America,* 128–40. Athens: University of Georgia Press, 1985.

Salter, Christopher L. "John Steinbeck's *The Grapes of Wrath* as a Primer for Cultural Geography." In *Humanistic Geography and Literature: Essays on the Experience of Place,* edited by Douglas C. Pocock, 142–58. London: Croom Helm, 1981.

Shockley, Martin Staples. "The Reception of *The Grapes of Wrath* in Oklahoma." *American Literature* 15 (1944): 351–61.

Slade, Leonard A., Jr. "The Use of Biblical Allusions in *The Grapes of Wrath.*" *CLA* 11 (1968): 241–47.

Taylor, Walter Fuller. "*The Grapes of Wrath* Reconsidered." *Mississippi Quarterly* 12 (1959): 136–44.

Tedlock, E. W., Jr., and C. V. Wicker, eds. *Steinbeck and His Critics.* Albuquerque: University of New Mexico Press, 1965.

Timmerman, John H. "The Wine of God's Wrath: *The Grapes of Wrath.*" In *John Steinbeck's Fiction: The Aesthetics of the Road Taken,* 102–32. Norman: University of Oklahoma Press, 1986.

Zollman, Sol. "John Steinbeck's Political Outlook in *The Grapes of Wrath.*" *Literature and Ideology* 13 (1972): 9–20.

Acknowledgments

"The Philosophical Joads" by Frederic I. Carpenter from *College English* 2, no. 4 (January 1941), © 1941 by the National Council of Teachers of English. Reprinted by permission of the publisher.

"The Fully Matured Art: *The Grapes of Wrath*" by Howard Levant from *The Novels of John Steinbeck: A Critical Study* by Howard Levant, © 1974 by the Curators of the University of Missouri. Reprinted by permission of the University of Missouri Press.

"*The Grapes of Wrath* and Old Testament Skepticism" by James D. Brasch from *San Jose Studies* 3, no. 2 (May 1977), © 1977 by James D. Brasch. Reprinted by permission

"Flat Wine from *The Grapes of Wrath*" by Floyd C. Watkins from *In Time and Place: Some Origins of American Fiction* by Floyd C. Watkins, © 1977 by the University of Georgia Press. Reprinted by permission of the University of Georgia Press.

"Steinbeck, the People, and the Party" by Sylvia Jenkins Cook from *Literature at the Barricades: The American Writer in the 1930s,* edited by Ralph F. Bogardus and Fred Hobson, © 1982 by the University of Alabama Press. Reprinted by permission.

"The Enduring Power of the Joads" (originally entitled "John Steinbeck: *The Grapes of Wrath*") by Donald Pizer from *Twentieth-Century American Literary Naturalism: An Interpretation* by Donald Pizer, © 1982 by Southern Illinois University Press. Reprinted by permission of the publisher and the author.

"Steinbeck and Nature's Self: *The Grapes of Wrath*" by John J. Conder from *Naturalism in American Fiction: The Classic Phase* by John J. Conder, © 1984 by the University Press of Kentucky. Reprinted by permission of the publisher.

"The Indestructible Women: Ma Joad and Rose of Sharon" (originally entitled "Steinbeck") by Mimi Reisel Gladstein from *The Indestructible Woman in Faulkner, Hemingway, and Steinbeck* by Mimi Reisel Gladstein, © 1974, 1986 by Mimi Reisel Gladstein. Reprinted by permission of UMI Research Press, Ann Arbor, Michigan.

Index

Hooper, Johnson Jones, 63
"How to Tell Good Guys from
     Bad Guys," 27
Huston, Ezra, 37, 38

In Dubious Battle, 1, 45; Doc
     Burton in, 37, 71, 74–75;
     Grapes of Wrath compared to,
     19, 20–21, 27, 35, 70, 72, 73,
     74, 76; the group in, 70–72,
     73, 76; Mac in, 71, 72, 75;
     themes of, 21, 22, 35, 38

James, Henry, 4
James, William, 8, 10, 13
Jim. *See* Casey, Jim or Rawley,
     Jim
Joad, Al: general characteristics of,
     29, 111–12; lustiness of, 11,
     12, 25, 126; selfishness of, 27,
     94
Joad, Grandma: death of, 26, 30,
     33, 34, 61, 94, 117;
     religious beliefs of, 25, 62
Joad, Grandpa: death of, 26, 29,
     32, 33, 61, 91, 94, 117;
     earthiness of, 11, 12, 25, 62;
     general characteristics of, 62,
     77
Joad, Ma: as mother figure, 118,
     125; as natural woman,
     88–89, 107, 118; philosophy
     of, 10, 21, 89; strength of, 25,
     29, 31, 39, 117–18, 119–21,
     125–26; as teacher, 121–22,
     123
Joad, Noah, 26, 94, 102
Joad, Pa, 25, 29, 62
Joad, Ruthie, 23, 30, 37, 42
Joad, Tom: general characteristics
     of, 24, 27, 40; Jim Casy and,
     11, 46–47; leadership of, 11,
     12, 24, 39, 105; moral
     development of, 20, 25,
     31–32, 75–76; as natural man,

88, 89; pragmatism of, 13, 14;
     as Saint Paul, 24–25, 39
Joad, Uncle John: guilt of, 25, 108;
     moral development of, 23, 27,
     113
Joad, Winfield, 23, 30, 42
John. *See* Joad, Uncle John
Johnson, James Weldon, 65
*John Steinbeck and Edward F.
     Ricketts: The Shaping of a
     Novelist* (Astro), 85

Koheleth, 46, 54

"Leader of the People, The," 72
Let Us Now Praise Famous Men
     (Agee), 80
Levant, Howard, 121, 124
Lewis, Sinclair, 62
Light in August (Faulkner), 62
Lisca, Peter, 33
Lizbeth, 107–8
Log from the Sea of Cortez, The,
     111
Lutwack, Leonard, 126

Ma. *See* Joad, Ma
McTeague (Norris), 113
McWilliams, Carey, 58–59
Madame Bovary (Flaubert), 41
Malory, Sir Thomas, 67
Manhattan Transfer (Dos Passos),
     103, 113
Marks, Lester Jay, 116
Marx, Karl, 11
Melville, Herman, 55
Milton, John, 45
Moby-Dick (Melville), 7, 65
Momaday, Scott, 58, 65
Mosquitoes (Faulkner), 65
Mr. Wainwright, 126
Mrs. Wilson, 27
Muley, 26, 77, 102

Noah, 26, 94, 102